# Sunday Rides

## on Two Wheels

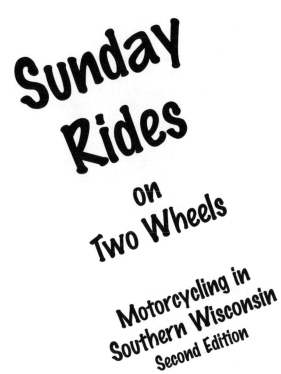

# Sunday Rides

## on
## Two Wheels

### Motorcycling in
### Southern Wisconsin
#### Second Edition

## with Barbara Barber

The University of Wisconsin Press

The University of Wisconsin Press
1930 Monroe Street, 3rd Floor
Madison, Wisconsin 53711-2059

www.wisc.edu/wisconsinpress/

3 Henrietta Street
London WC2E 8LU, England

5     4     3     2

Printed in the United States of America

The Library of Congress has cataloged the first edition as follows:
Barber, Barbara, 1948–
Sunday Rides on two wheels: motorcycling in southern Wisconsin / Barbara Barber.
        p.       cm
ISBN 0-299-18454-4 (pbk.: alk. paper)
1. Motorcycling—Wisconsin—Guidebooks. 2. Wisconsin—Guidebooks. I. Title.
GV1059.522.W6 B37        2003
796.7'5—dc21        2002074036

Second edition ISBN: 978-0-299-23024-1 (pbk.: alk. paper)

# CONTENTS

# INTRODUCTION

I'm old enough to remember when a Sunday ride was the family's afternoon entertainment. My dad would pack us into the sedan and we'd head out on to rural roads for a leisurely drive in the countryside. Sitting in the back seat, the wind would blow through my hair and the sun would shine on me through the windows. Now my Sunday riding is done on a motorcycle. And even though my ride may take place on a Tuesday, it still has a Sunday ride feel — the leisurely pace, the sun on my head, the wind in my face, and the sense of exploration — riding for the love of riding.

And I do love to ride. As evidence of that, I've put over 200,000 miles on my Harleys® in the last ten years. I also like planning my routes (it's nearly as much fun as riding) so it seemed a perfect match to use my two passions to put together a travel book. **Sunday Rides** contains over 1,800 miles of some of the best riding in southern Wisconsin that you can do any day of the week.

I can't resist a good road whether riding along and spotting a side road with a visible bend or seeing two inches of curvy line on a map. For the most part this has been a good thing, but on occasion I've wound up on some unpleasant dirt or gravel. In this book you will find good side roads and curvy lines without concern for gravel and dirt. Because you'd rather be riding, I've done the planning for you and provided the maps and directions.

Since you've purchased this book, you're probably looking for new places to ride. The routes I've selected may take you to destinations you know, but there are back roads you may not have ridden or even known about. I've started many of the rides from small towns because they're centrally located to the route and also they're totally charming places to spend a weekend. You may wish to start the routes at any point convenient to you.

This book is for motorcyclists of both sexes, but as a woman, I'm also writing this to encourage more women to venture out on their own. I ride solo much of the time, and I hope my little anecdotes and descriptions will be of value. Safety is always a concern, especially for women, so the establishments mentioned are family friendly. I would not hesitate to enter them alone.

## HOW TO USE THIS BOOK

I've divided southern Wisconsin into five sections. Each section begins with an overview of the geologic features that make the riding interesting. The overview may also include historical background of the region's settlement.

Each region contains two to five routes. The route description includes:

- ◆ General overview of the area covered on the route.
- ◆ Highlights and special notes about things along the way.
- ◆ Maps. Legend:
  - ▨ – streams, rivers, & lakes;
  - ▨ – forests, prairies, & marshes;
  - ▦ – cities, villages, & towns.
  
  The cities are named, but the lakes are not.
- ◆ Directions.
- ◆ Listing of websites and phone numbers for more information on area attractions.
- ◆ Representative photos to say what I never could.

Whether you ride on Sunday or any other day, I hope you will find the routes interesting and that some will become your favorites to ride again and again.

Now . . . get out and enjoy the road!

Barbara Barber
September 2008

# ACKNOWLEDGMENTS

*Sunday Rides on Two Wheels* was first published in 2003, and the good people at Uke's Harley-Davidson have been my biggest supporters. Heather, Liz, Bree, Nicole, and Terry, thanks for putting my book in front of everyone who walks in the door. Larisa and Wally, thanks for getting my bike on the service schedule. And Ray, "you da man!" Not only are you a terrific mechanic, you're a great friend. Keith and Nanc, if it wasn't for you, I'd never have gotten out of the garage. You all truly make me feel like family.

Thanks to the members of the Kenosha HOG® chapter, who have been a great source of inspiration and encouragement.

I have two really good friends, Cindy Baffa and Jackie Nelson, who helped with the nitty gritty of editing. They both spent countless hours critiquing the book and agonizing about my feelings with every pencil mark. I thank them both for not letting our friendship get in the way.

And finally, many thanks to Mike Bielenda, Jeff Dickson, Elm Lake Cranberry Company, Jean Knuesel, and Marion Wagner for helping me out with photographic duties. Their time and efforts were invaluable.

Ralph & Baxter waiting for a ride

# I - GLACIER COUNTRY

**BREAKFAST AT MILLIE'S - 86 MILES**
**ROADS OFF HIGHWAY 20 - 67 MILES**
**LAKE COUNTRY - 88 MILES**
**RUSTIC ROADS - 143 MILES**
**BREAKOUT RIDE 2000 - 100 MILES**

# I - GLACIER COUNTRY

Southeast Wisconsin is noted for its proximity to Lake Michigan and for the Milwaukee/Chicago corridor. Once west of I-94 though, there are a surprising number of rural, scenic roads, thanks to the Wisconsin Glacier.

It seems odd in this day when we worry about global warming to remember that 14,000 years ago Wisconsin was covered with a mile-thick sheet of ice. The effects of glacial advances and retreats are well preserved in the state in general and in southeastern Wisconsin especially. Southwestern Wisconsin was untouched by the glacier and provides the "before" picture.

Glaciers had such power that they could reduce mountains to bedrock. The resulting debris (drift) that was carried along was deposited as parallel hills and ridges (moraines). The glacial drift was deposited repeatedly, marking both the glaciers' advance as well as retreat over thousands of years. Moraines were created by the ice itself as it pushed debris forward. As the glacier melted and receded, the water had torrential strength. It cut canyons and potholes (kettles) and deposited debris in cone-shaped hills (kames) and snake-like ridges (eskers). The fieldstone found in Wisconsin fences and fireplaces is not from here originally, but is actually drift from Canada.

Because the glacier both gouged and filled depressions and left mounds of debris, the natural drainage patterns in southeastern

Produce stand on Hwy 20

Wisconsin were disrupted. This resulted in a large number of lakes and an even larger number of bogs and marshes as old lakes drained and streams were blocked.

Although Wisconsin winters often feel glacial,

the last ice age ended 10,000 years ago. Fortunately, we are able to enjoy the hills, bogs, marshes, and lakes left behind in all seasons, although I find it particularly ironic to ride the motorcycle by the lakes when people are out ice fishing.

There are five routes totaling 484 miles in the **Glacier Country** section:

- *Breakfast at Millie's*
- *Roads off Highway 20*
- *Lake Country*
- *Rustic Roads*
- *Breakout Ride 2000*

The five routes start west of Racine at the junction of I-94 and Highway 20, or west of Kenosha at the junction of I-94 and Highway 50.

Mailbox - Loomis Rd./R-5

Millie's Pancake Haus

*Breakfast at Millie's is* one of my favorite routes, particularly on a hot day. It winds around and through several lake resorts where there are cool breezes and tree canopies. You will pass little lakes such as Lake Tombeau and big lakes like Geneva Lake. Houses along the way vary in size as well, from simple cottages to magnificent mansions. For the most part the roads on this route are unhurried, so you can enjoy the curves and twists and scenery. The busiest sections are the south shores of both Geneva Lake and Lake Delavan. Here the passenger is the lucky one to be able to watch the scenery and comment, "Wow, look at that house!"

## NOTES & HIGHLIGHTS

*Breakfast at Millie's* starts west of Kenosha at the intersection of Highway 50 and Interstate 94. There are several gas stations and restaurants: McDonalds, Subway, Taco Bell, KFC, Phoenix Family Restaurant, and the famous Brat Stop.

County Road F is a fun road with nice, easy curves and two of Kenosha County's fine parks: Silver Lake and Fox River. Both offer a chance to sit along the river to relax and enjoy the water. Also along County F are the Swartz nursery and the village of Bassett.

93rd Street divides Powers Lake on the right and Benedict Lake on the left. Tombeau Road winds along the west edge of Benedict Lake and through Nippersink Golf Course. The road here is twisty and narrow amid almost fairy tale–like cottages.

While the route does not go through the city of Lake Geneva, it is easy to make a detour by turning right on South Lake Shore Drive instead of left. You will find plenty of souvenirs, gifts, food, ice cream, and, of course, people in Lake Geneva on a summer weekend.

By following the route on South Lake Shore Drive, you will pass Big Foot Beach State Park. This little strip of picnic area on one side of the road and beach on the other was purchased from Fred Maytag of home appliance fame. It is one of a few public access points to the lake and is very popular with swimmers, sunbathers, and boaters who tie up close to shore to enjoy the beach and party scene. The route south of the lake gives an idea of the immense wealth that has flocked to Lake Geneva since the late 1800s, when Lake Geneva was called the "Newport of the

Ice boats on Geneva Lake - Fontana

West." The largest mansion along the lake was built by Otto Young in 1900–1901 for the price of one million dollars. It has recently been restored and converted into six condominiums. As you ride through this area, marvel that land cost $1.25 an acre in 1839.

No one will mistake Millie's Restaurant for Tiffany's, but breakfast at Millie's is better than the movie. Millie's, located on the corner of County O and South Shore Road, has been a part of the Lake Delavan area since 1964. Judging by the parking lot on Sunday morning, it will continue. There are other menu choices, but pancakes are the specialty of the house. In addition to good food, Millie's has several gift shops to make the weekend wait less painful. In the past, Millie's accepted only cash or check in the restaurant, but you can now come armed with your MasterCard or Visa.

Krueger, Buckby, Spring Valley, and Walburg Roads are nice rolling rural roads through woods and farmland. As an added attraction along Walburg, you will see the vehicle proving grounds originally built by American Motors. County Roads W, K, and NN offer a diversion from Highway 50 with a few nice curves thrown in.

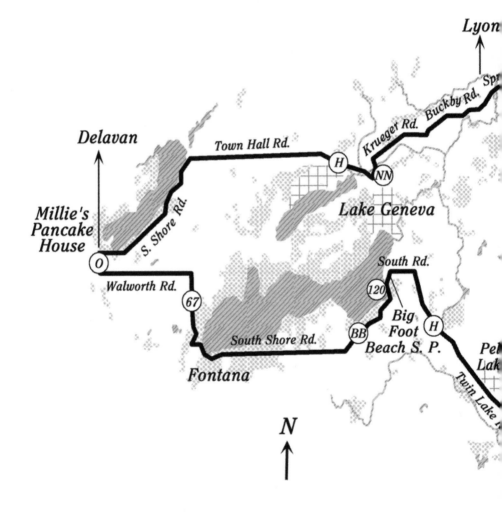

Lyon

Spr

Krueger Rd.  Buckby Rd.

Delavan

Town Hall Rd.

H

NN

Lake Geneva

Millie's
Pancake
House

S. Shore Rd.

O

South Rd.

Walworth Rd.

67

120

Big
Foot
Beach S. P.

H

Pel
Lak

BB

South Shore Rd.

Fontana

Twin Lake

N

# BREAKFAST AT MILLIE'S
## 86 MILES

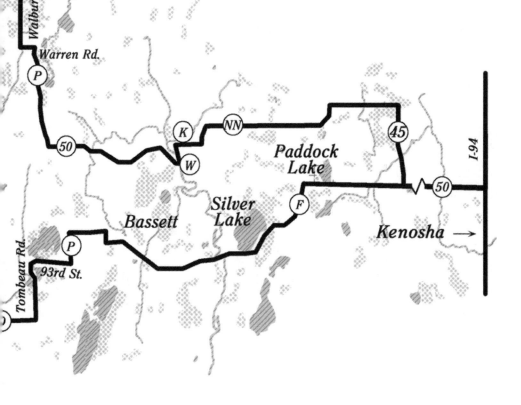

# BREAKFAST AT MILLIE'S - 86 MILES

Start west of Kenosha. Gas up at one of the four gas stations at the intersection of I-94 and Hwy 50.

| Road | Direction | | Miles |
|---|---|---|---|
| Hwy 50 | | W | 9.8 |
| County F | Left | SW | 3.8 |
| County P | Left | S | .7 |
| 93rd St. | Right | W | 1.4 |
| Tombeau Rd./400th Ave. | Left | S | 2.3 |
| County O/110th Rd. | Right | W | 1.5 |
| Twin Lake Rd. | Straight | W | 1.2 |
| County H | Right | N | 5.4 |
| South Rd. | Left | W | .9 |
| S. Lake Shore Rd. | Left | S | 1.2 |
| County BB | Right | SW | 1.6 |
| South Shore Rd./Fontana Blvd. | Right | W | 5.9 |
| Hwy 67 | Right | N | 1.9 |
| Walworth Rd. | Left | W | 3.4 |
| County O | Right | N | .5 |
| S. Shore Rd. | Right | E | 4.7 |
| Town Hall Rd./Palmer Rd. | Straight | E | 4.8 |
| County H | Right | SE | 2.2 |
| County NN | Left | N | .5 |
| Krueger Rd./Buckby Rd. | Right | E | 4.4 |
| Spring Valley Rd. | Left | E | 2.8 |
| Walburg Rd. | Right | S | 1.0 |
| Warren Rd. | Left | E | .5 |
| County P/McHenry St. | Right | S | 2.6 |
| Hwy 50 | Left | E | 4.9 |
| County W | Left | N | .6 |
| County K | Right | E | .9 |
| County NN | Left | NE | 7.7 |
| Hwy 45 | Right | S | 2.0 |
| Hwy 50 | Left | E | 4.6 |

# FOR MORE INFORMATION

**Big Foot Beach State Park** (state park sticker required)
262-248-2528
www.dnr.wi.gov/org/land/parks/specific/bigfoot

**Kenosha**
Convention & Visitor's Bureau 800-654-7309
www.kenoshacvb.com
Bristol Renaissance Faire 847-395-7773 www.renfair.com/bristol
summer weekends, call for dates
Jelly Belly Candy Co. 800-522-3267 www.jellybelly.com
Tours daily, exc. major holidays
Russell Military Museum 847-395-7020
www.russellmilitarymuseum.com
Uke's Harley-Davidson/Buell 262-857-8537 www.ukeshd.com

**Lyons**
Ye Olde Hotel Bar & Restaurant 262-763-2701

**Lake Geneva**
Chamber of Commerce 800-345-1020 or 262-248-4416
www.lakegenevawi.com
Millie's Restaurant 262-728-2434 www.millieswis.com
Closed Mondays/January & February—open weekends

**Williams Bay**
Yerkes Observatory 262-245-5555 ext. 832
http://astro.uchicago.edu/yerkes/visiting/index.html
Tours on Saturdays 10 a.m., 11 a.m., & noon

---

One of the biggest fears of beginning motorcycle riders is that they'll drop their bikes. This most always happens while the bike is standing still, so I figure drop it and get it over with. It seems three is my magic number. Every new bike I get, I manage to drop it three times in the first few months. I dropped my current bike three times on one trip, although the trip was 7,100 miles long so I figure that's not so bad. A sense of humor is always a good accessory when this happens. After all, there are those who have dropped their bikes and those who will.

# 2  ROADS OFF HIGHWAY 20

*Roads off Highway 20* passes through open farmland as well as woods and apple orchards. The area is crisscrossed by numerous creeks and marshes. The county highways are usually in good shape, but many of the local roads are more like lanes. They are narrow, hilly, and twisty, providing their own interest along with the scenery. Take special caution if you ride in the early spring. Many of these areas use sand instead of road salt in the winter. It is still on the roads in springtime, making corners slippery.

Highway 20 connects Racine to East Troy between I-94 and I-43. It is a fast, well-maintained route with both tight turns and sweeping curves through marshes and farmland and the growing community of Waterford. At typical rush hour periods in morning and evening it is a busy highway, but the rest of the day it is less well traveled. It is a pleasurable ride all by itself or as a conduit to some of the backroads of western Racine County and eastern Walworth County.

You can use this guide to travel a circuitous route over the back roads, or you can shoot out Highway 20 and take portions of the route. Directions are written to tour the entire route.

## NOTES & HIGHLIGHTS

*Roads off Highway 20* starts west of Racine at the intersection of Highway 20 and Interstate 94, where you will find McDonalds, Burger King, Culvers, and Iron Skillet. Spokes Restaurant & Bar is a popular spot for motorcyclists—check out their mural. There are several gas stations also. Nearby is the Ives Grove Golf Course. A little farther down the road is Evans Park. It is a great place for a picnic if you want to bring your fast food lunch to a secluded, quiet little park.

At the corner of Highway 20 and County Road S is a tavern called the Dover Inn that serves lunch, dinner, and pleasant company.

The countryside along Dover Line Road is a nice sample of rural character with its farm houses, open fields, and woodlots. If you ride in early spring, watch for sandhill cranes in the freshly plowed fields and along the marshes. The sandhill is quite tall with a red forehead.

Waterford is a booming little village with a number of gift shops and cafes. Uncle Harry's is a popular spot for custard.

As you travel through the township of Honey Creek take note of the spectacular home on the ridge seen from both Honey Creek Road and Bell School Road. Owned by an Illinois financier, it is a vacation home. Also look for the wonderful stone house and old barn on Colbo Road.

County D just west of Rochester is an easy, curvy road and is a favorite fall color destination. Autumn is also the time for apples and cider at the Ela Orchard. This family-run business is in its third generation. They grow thirty varieties of apples as well as sheep and friendly goats.

The small town of Rochester, home to author Jane Hamilton, is a gift shopper's delight and well worth the stop. You can't help but take home something from Angel Acres or Finder's Keepers. Chances Tavern offers a nice menu for lunch or dinner. Enjoy a cup of joe at Stir Crazy Coffee. A nice, peaceful, little park nestles along the Fox River at the corner of County Roads W and C.

German Settlement Church - County D

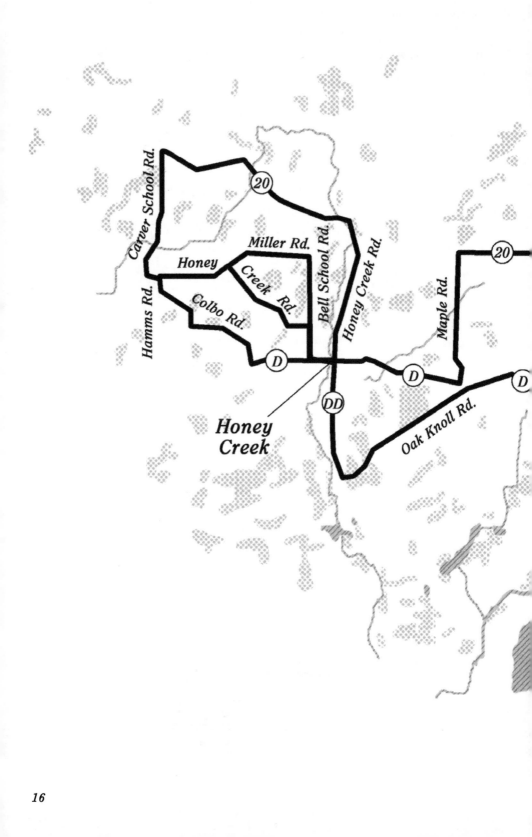

# ROADS OFF
# HIGHWAY 20
## 67 MILES

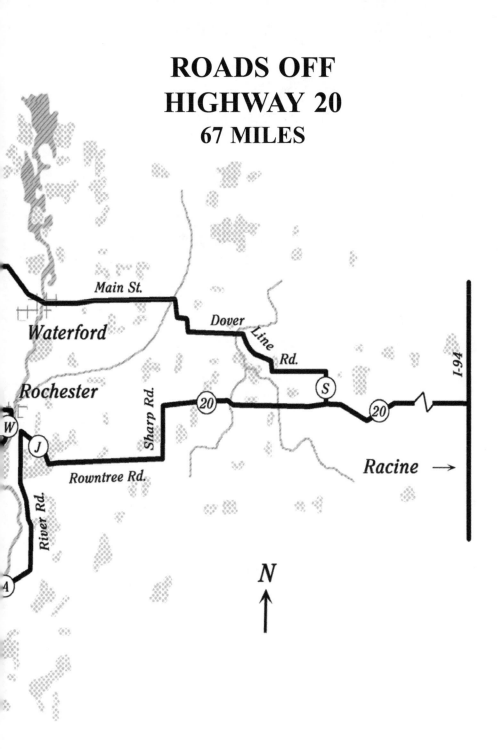

# ROADS OFF HIGHWAY 20 - 67 MILES

Start west of Racine. Gas up at one of the four gas stations at the intersection of I-94 and Hwy 20.

| Road | Direction | | Miles |
|------|-----------|---|-------|
| Hwy 20 | | W | 8.1 |
| County S | Right | N | 0.5 |
| Dover Line Rd./Main St. | Left | W | 5.9 |
| Hwy 20 | Straight | W | 3.1 |
| Maple Rd. (Rustic Rd.) | Left | S | 1.8 |
| County D | Right | W | 2.4 |
| Honey Creek Rd. | Right | N | 1.4 |
| Hwy 20 | Left | W | 4.0 |
| Carver School Rd. | Left | S | 1.9 |
| Honey Creek Rd. | Left | E | 0.2 |
| Hamms Rd. | Right | S | 0.2 |
| Colbo Rd. | Left | SE | 2.1 |
| County D | Left | E | 1.0 |
| Bell School Rd. | Left | N | 0.5 |
| Honey Creek Rd. | Left | NW | 1.7 |
| Miller Rd. | Right | W | 1.3 |
| Bell School Rd. | Right | S | 1.5 |
| County D | Left | E | 0.5 |
| County DD | Right | S | 1.6 |
| Oak Knoll Rd. (Rustic Road) | Left | NE | 2.6 |
| County D via Rochester | Right | E | 2.0 |
| County W | Right | S | 3.0 |
| County A | Left | E | 1.1 |
| River Rd. | Left | N | 2.1 |
| County J/English Settlement Rd. | Right | SE | 0.8 |
| Rowntree Rd. | Left | E | 2.1 |
| Sharp Rd. | Left | N | 0.7 |

# FOR MORE INFORMATION

### Racine
Racine County Convention & Visitor's Bureau 800-272-2463
www.racine.org
Apple Holler Restaurant 262-884-7100 www.appleholler.com
Borzynski's Farm Market 262-886-2235 www.borzynskis.com
Spokes Restaurant & Bar 262-898-7900

### Rochester
Angel Acres 262-534-7300
Chances Tavern 262-534-2772
Ela Orchard 262-534-2545
Finders Keepers 262-534-9298
Stir Crazy Coffee & Bakery 262-534-1929

### Waterford
Chamber of Commerce 262-534-5911 www.waterford-wi.org/
Green Meadows Petting Farm 262-534-2891
www.greenmeadowsfarmwi.com
Summer only. Sat. & Sun. Call for hours
Hoppe Homestead Family Dairy Farm 262-534-6480
May–Oct. Call for hours
Uncle Harry's Ice Cream  262-534-4757

Riding solo, especially for a woman, can be a daunting experience whether it's a first time trip around the block or one across the country. Before a trip, I'm usually so preoccupied with preparations that I don't have much time to think about the adventure ahead. It's when I stand back and look at the bike all loaded that the butterflies start to flutter in my stomach. The anticipation of the journey is nearly palpable and I find it hard to contain my anxiety. This feeling stays with me as I ride down the driveway and out into the street. It's when I reach the highway that the anxiety seems to float away with the wind in my face, and I can't help yelling an internal, "Yee-ha!"

# 3  LAKE COUNTRY

*Lake Country* is wonderful in the heat of summer because it passes through residential areas bustling with lake activity as well as through areas that are less traveled. The smell of charcoal grills, the mist of sprinklers on the sod farms, the slow glide of a redtail hawk, and the stick figure of a heron will all greet you. This route combines both roads that satisfy the need for speed as well as those that are more laid back. Many are tree lined, with overhanging branches creating a canopy to give much welcomed shade.

## NOTES & HIGHLIGHTS

*Lake Country* starts west of Racine at the intersection of Highway 20 and Interstate 94 where you will find McDonalds, Burger King, Culvers, Iron Skillet, and Spokes Restaurant & Bar. There are several gas stations also.

Much of southeastern Wisconsin is still engaged in farming, and the usual crops are corn and soybeans. In the area between North Cape and Wind Lake, the crop is shorter and greener—sod. At least five sod companies call this area home.

The ride along the south and west sides of Wind Lake will take you past tiny cottages as well as larger, newer year-round residences that cover nearly every inch of the lakeside property. The road twists and turns as it follows the contours of the lake before opening up to Highway 36. This four lane highway will take you north to Milwaukee or south to Burlington, but you will want to cross it to connect with Loomis Road which is a part of the Rustic Road system.

The Tichigan area is not as busy as Wind Lake and has more open lake and meadow. A local landmark is the Tichigan Tower gas station, built in 1934 with a red tile roof. Bridge Drive is a popular fishing spot, and if you are lucky, you may see the mute swans that are occasional visitors there.

County Road L takes you out of the lake area, and you can enjoy open vistas and highway speeds. You will pass through Lake Beulah which, ironically, is not located on Beulah Lake. The turn at Stone School Road is marked most distinctly by a big red barn, and you will take the road sharply to the right.

You will get a chance to see Beulah Lake when you get to East

Shore Road. Dockside Grog & Galley offers excellent views of the lake and good food. Although this road is only a mile long, it offers a climbing, twisting path under a canopy of branches. It also seemed like a step back in time when I came upon a horse and carriage taking its occupants for a romantic ride.

From East Shore Road, you will go only a half mile to Marsh Road, which is partially obscured and easy to miss. This is a nice lightly traveled road through marshes and some woodlands. Mukwonago Park is located on County LO just east of the intersection of Marsh Road and LO (former Hwy 99). It is a very pleasant park with a beach and picnic area as well as a campground.

If you are in need of gas or food, stay on County E to the intersection of County LO. You will find a country store as well as a tavern and a pizza place. Continuing on E is a fun stretch of road along Booth Lake.

Rochester is an active little town. You will find a farmer's market in the summer and fall and special community events throughout the year. Stop and say "hi" to Brian at Angel Acres and Tracy at Finders Keepers. Chances Tavern offers good food and cold drinks. Nancy and Frank enjoy talking with all their motorcycling customers at Stir Crazy Coffee.

Beulah Lake

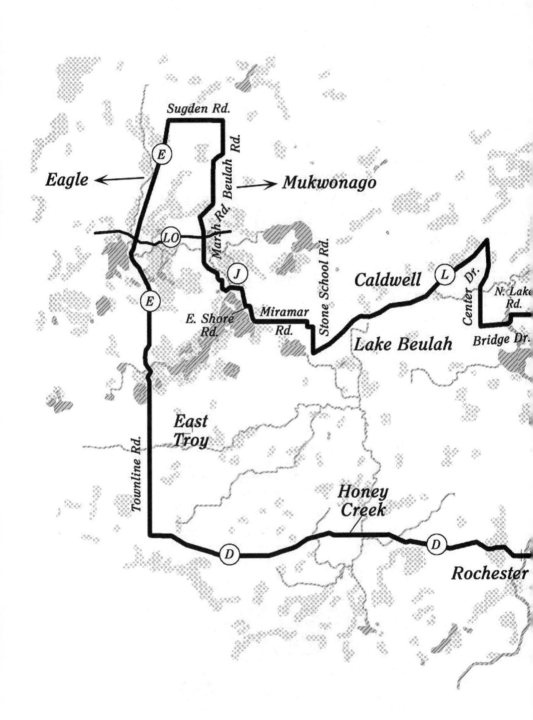

Sugden Rd.

(E)

Eagle ←

Marsh Rd.

Beulah Rd.

→ Mukwonago

(LO)

(J)

Stone School Rd.

Caldwell

(L)

Center Dr.

N. Lake Rd.

(E)

E. Shore Rd.

Miramar Rd.

Lake Beulah

Bridge Dr.

East Troy

Townline Rd.

Honey Creek

(D)

(D)

Rochester

# LAKE COUNTRY
## 88 MILES

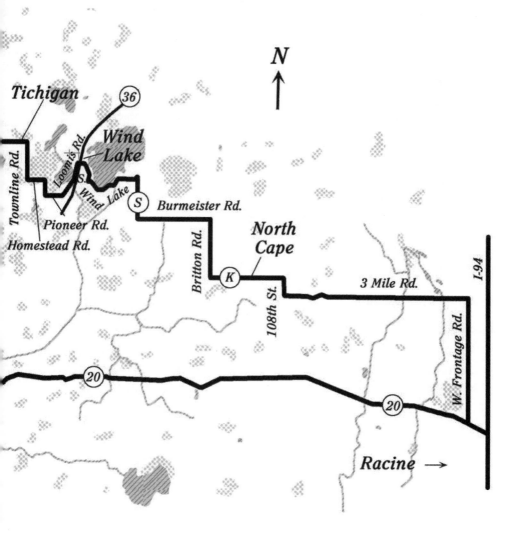

# LAKE COUNTRY - 88 MILES

Start west of Racine. Gas up at one of the four gas stations at the intersection of I-94 and Hwy 20.

| Road | Direction | | Miles |
|------|-----------|---|-------|
| W. Frontage Rd. | | N | 3.0 |
| 3 Mile Rd. | Left | W | 5.0 |
| 108th St. | Right | N | 0.5 |
| County K | Left | W | 1.9 |
| Britton Rd./Burmeister Rd. | Right | N | 3.5 |
| County S | Right | N | 1.2 |
| S. Wind Lake Rd. | Left | W | 2.0 |
| Loomis Rd. | Left | S | 1.0 |
| Pioneer Rd./Homestead Rd. | Right | W | 1.3 |
| Townline Rd./N. Lake Rd. | Right | N | 3.7 |
| Bridge Dr. | Left | S | 0.5 |
| Center Dr. | Right | N | 2.3 |
| County L | Left | W | 5.8 |
| Stone School Rd. | Right | N | 0.5 |
| Miramar Rd. | Left | W | 0.9 |
| Cross County ES | Straight | W | 0.9 |
| E. Shore Rd. | Right | N | 1.0 |
| County J | Left | W | 0.5 |
| Marsh Rd./Beulah Rd. | Right | N | 4.9 |
| Sugden Rd. | Left | W | 1.5 |
| County E | Left | S | 11.0 |
| County D | Left | E | 10.2 |
| Hwy 20 | Right | E | 14.2 |

# FOR MORE INFORMATION

**Eagle**

    Old World Wisconsin  262-594-6300
        www.oldworldwisconsin.org
        May–October, fee

**East Troy**

    Chamber of Commerce 262-642-3770
        www.easttroywi.org
    Alpine Valley Music Theatre 262-642-4400
    Buell Motorcycle Company 262-642-2020 Call about tours
    East Troy Electric Railroad 262-642-3263 Summer only
        www.easttroyrr.org
    Elegant Farmer 262-363-6770 www.elegantfarmer.com
    Lauber's Old Fashioned Ice Cream Parlor 262-642-3679
    Gus's Drive-In 262-642-2929 www.gussdrivein.com

**Racine**

    Racine County Convention & Visitor's Bureau 800-272-2463
        www.racine.org
    Apple Holler Restaurant 262-884-7100 www.appleholler.com
    Borzynski's Farm Market 262-886-2235 www.borzynskis.com
    Spokes Restaurant & Bar 262-898-7900

**Rochester**

    Angel Acres 262-534-7300
    Chances Tavern 262-534-2772
    Ela Orchard 262-534-2545
    Finders Keepers 262-534-9298
    Stir Crazy Coffee & Bakery 262-534-1929

---

Many visitors to this part of the state laugh when we mention hills, but I had an interesting experience with one of the "hills" while taking photos on Bowers Road. I parked the motorcycle on a little turnoff and walked down the road to shoot. When I turned back, I nearly died when I saw my bike had rolled backwards in a semicircle on the kickstand and was sitting in the middle of the road. Yes, we have hills.

# 4  RUSTIC ROADS

Rustic Roads were first created by the Wisconsin Legislature in 1973. There are currently 103 roads throughout the state, with a large share (27) located in the southeastern section. Racine, Kenosha, and Walworth Counties have 13 of the roads.

In order to be designated a Rustic Road, there must be natural features such as rugged terrain, wildlife areas, or agricultural views that edge the roadway and make it unique. The Rustic Roads are generally lightly traveled. These roads of two miles or more can be paved, dirt, or gravel. All of the roads featured here are paved. The maximum speed is 45 m.p.h., but each locality can set speeds as low as 25 m.p.h.

Each Rustic Road begins with the letter "R" and is numbered as it is designated. Brown and yellow signs are used to indicate the Rustic Road

Rustic Road sign

system. The State of Wisconsin puts out an exceptional publication titled *Wisconsin's Rustic Roads: A Positive Step Backward*. This booklet describes each road and its location and may be obtained for free by contacting:

> The Rustic Road Program
> Wisconsin Department of Transportation
> P.O. Box 7913
> Madison, Wisconsin 53707-7913
> 608-267-7753

## RUSTIC ROAD MOTORCYCLE TOUR

This special program is sponsored by the Wisconsin Department of Transportation—Motorcycle Safety Program. A rider receives a patch for traveling ten Rustic Roads or a certificate for 25 roads. To verify this feat, a picture must be taken of the rider with his or her motorcycle in front of the

German Settlement Cemetery - County D

numbered Rustic Road sign. Once the required number of pictures is obtained, the rider sends them to the Motorcycle Safety Program. For more information or to forward the required photos, contact:

Wisconsin Motorcycle Safety Program
Bureau of Transportation Safety
P.O. Box 7936
Madison, Wisconsin 53707-7936
800-368-9677

The Rustic Roads tour in this book is designed so that the rider may travel ten roads and be eligible for the patch.

## NOTES & HIGHLIGHTS

I enjoy a scenic road, but I prefer one that also has nice curves. The following meet that criteria:

R-37 (3 Mile Road) has more houses now, but has not had its basic course changed since it was laid out in the early 1800s.

R-85 (Kearney Road) is not in the best repair, but it runs along one of the glacial ridges in the area.

R-2 is made up of three parts: Maple Lane, Heritage Road, and Maple Drive. I like Maple Lane between County FF and Burlington best because of its curves and overhanging canopy of trees. There is a wonderful old stone house at the corner of Heritage Road and County D.

Cow mailbox - Loomis Rd./R-5

The roads that make up R-11 and R-36 are some of my favorites. Steele Road and Knob Hill Road offer some nice hills that can get you airborne if taken too fast. Cranberry Road and Berndt Road are a challenge to ride and just plain pretty as they swoop up and around the hills. You can't help notice the glacial topography. Cranberry Road was named after the many cranberry bogs that dotted the area at one time.

R-12 runs from Highway 50 to the town of Lyons and includes Back Road, Sheridan Springs Road, Spring Valley Road and Church Road. Back Road is a must for anyone who likes sharp curves. Area riders gravitate to it at least once a summer. Ye Olde Hotel in Lyons offers an excellent lunch or dinner. The buffalo stew is especially hearty.

R-29 (Snake Road) is described as being located in "the countryside of natural and unspoiled beauty." While you are noticing the natural beauty, you will be awed by the wealthy estates bordering this road. In addition, the narrow, twisting road will hone your driving skills.

You will find places for food in Waterford, Rochester, Burlington, Lyons, and Lake Geneva. There are no gas stations in Rochester.

Back Rd./R-12 - Lyons

Pumpkin harvest - County D

I love to ride no matter what the season.

Winter rides are amazing. After weeks of dull, gray skies, snowstorms, and freezing temperatures, magic occurs. The sun rises bright and warm and the frost evaporates from the roads. The sky is clear, bright blue, and I just have to get on the bike. Even if it's for a ride around the block, the day is too perfect not to ride.

Spring is that great time of awakening, especially for those who have stored their bikes for the winter. Why is it 50 degrees suddenly seems so warm?

Summer, of course, is prime time. For me, the hotter the better. It's a good excuse to ride and never stop.

Fall riding days are gifts. All my household chores are put on hold because well, maybe, this will be the last "nice" day. And what other season offers destinations to caramel apples, pumpkins, apple cider, and trees bursting with spectacular color.

# RUSTIC ROADS
## 143 MILES

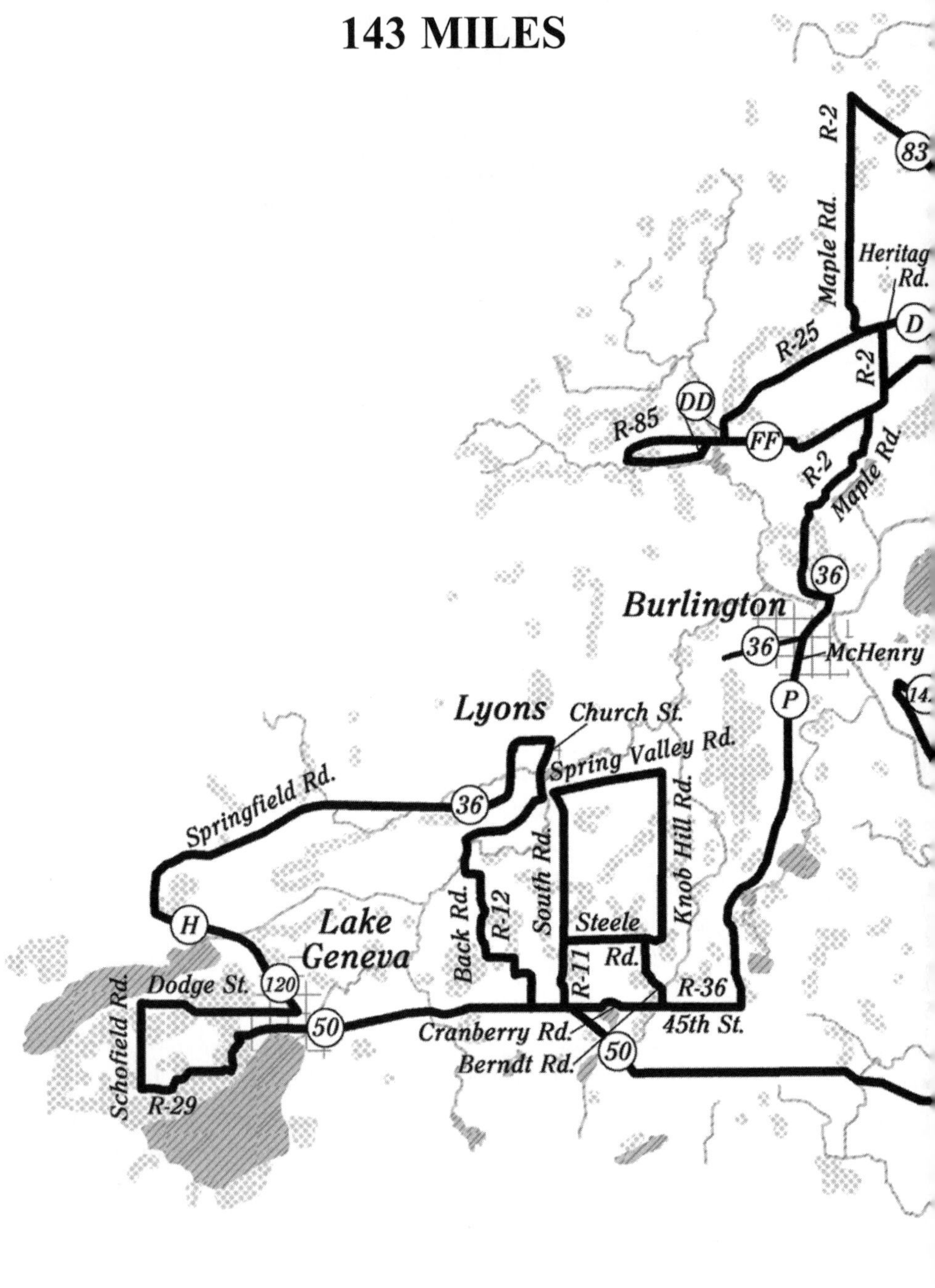

R-2

83

Maple Rd.

Heritag Rd.

R-25

D

R-2

R-85

DD

FF

R-2

Maple Rd.

36

Burlington

36

McHenry

P

14.

Lyons

Church St.

Spring Valley Rd.

Springfield Rd.

36

Knob Hill Rd.

Back Rd.

R-12

South Rd.

Steele Rd.

H

Lake
Geneva

R-11

R-36

Schofield Rd.

Dodge St.

120

50

45th St.

Cranberry Rd.

50

R-29

Berndt Rd.

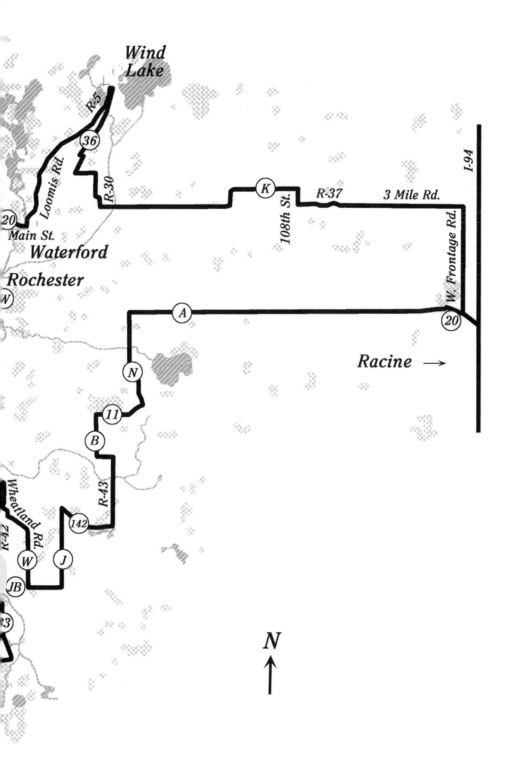

Wind Lake

R-5

36

R-30

Loomis Rd.

20

Main St.

Waterford

Rochester

W

K

108th St.

R-37

3 Mile Rd.

I-94

W. Frontage Rd.

A

Racine →

20

N

11

B

R-43

Wheatland Rd.

142

K-74

W

J

JB

3

N
↑

# RUSTIC ROADS - 143 MILES

Start west of Racine. Gas up at one of the four gas stations at the intersection of I-94 and Hwy 20.

| Road | Direction | | Miles |
|------|-----------|---|-------|
| West Frontage Rd. | | N | 3.0 |
| 3 Mile Rd. | Left | W | 3.2 |
| Becomes R-37 | Straight | W | 1.8 |
| 108th St. | Right | N | 0.5 |
| County K | Left | W | 6.2 |
| R-30 (Hillcrest Rd.) | Right | N | 2.3 |
| Hwy 36 | Right | N | 2.2 |
| R-5 (Fries Ln./Loomis Rd.) | Left | S | 3.1 |
| Continues as Loomis Rd. | Straight | S | 1.3 |
| Becomes Milwaukee St. | Straight | S | 0.7 |
| Main St. via Waterford | Right | W | 0.1 |
| Becomes Hwy 20/83 | Straight | NW | 1.3 |
| Hwy 83 | Right | NW | 2.4 |
| R-2 (Maple Rd.) | Left | S | 3.5 |
| County D | Left | E | 0.2 |
| R-25 (Oak Knoll Dr.) | Right | W | 2.5 |
| County DD | Left | S | 0.6 |
| R-85 (Kearney Rd.) | Right | W | 2.5 |
| County DD | Left | N | 0.5 |
| County FF via Rochester | Straight | E | 4.5 |
| County W | Left | N | 0.2 |
| County D | Left | E | 1.9 |
| R-2 (Heritage Rd.) | Left | S | 0.9 |
| County FF | Right | W | 0.5 |
| R-2 (Maple Rd./Honey Lake) | Left | S | 3.5 |
| Hwy 36 in Burlington | Right | S | 2.8 |
| McHenry St./County P | Left | S | 6.0 |
| | Triangle corner—busy intersection | | |
| R-36 (45th St./Cranberry Rd.) | Right | W | 2.7 |
| | First right after County sign | | |

| Road | Direction | | Miles |
|---|---|---|---|
| Hwy 50 | Right | W | 0.1 |
| R-11 (South Rd.) | Right | N | 1.0 |
| R-11 (Steele Rd./Knob Hill Rd.) | Right | E/N | 4.0 |
| R-11 (Spring Valley Rd.) | Left | W | 1.6 |
| R-11 (South Rd.) | Left | S | 2.2 |
| R-11 (Steele Rd.) | Left | E | 1.3 |
| R-36 (Berndt Rd.) | Right | S | 1.1 |
| R-36 (Cranberry Rd.) | Right | W | 1.4 |
| Hwy 50 | Right | W | 0.6 |
| R-12 (Back Rd.) via Lyons | Right | N | 5.7 |
| Hwy 36 | Left | W | 3.5 |
| Springfield Rd. | Straight | W | 4.1 |
| County H | Left | SE | 2.6 |
| Williams St. | Right | S | 0.3 |
| Dodge St./Mcdonald Rd. | Right | W | 2.4 |
| Schofield Rd. | Left | S | 0.7 |
| R-29 | Straight | SE | 2.7 |
| Hwy 50 via Lake Geneva | Right | E | 12.3 |
| Hwy 83 | Left | N | 2.2 |
| County JB | Right | E | 0.2 |
| R-42 (Hoosier Crk./Brever Rd.) | Left | N | 4.7 |
| Hwy 142 | Right | E | 1.8 |
| County W/Wheatland Rd. | Right | S | 3.4 |
| County JB | Left | E | 1.0 |
| County J | Left | N | 2.2 |
| Hwy 142 | Right | E | 1.7 |
| R-43/County B | Left | N | 3.7 |
| Hwy 11 | Right | E | 1.4 |
| County N | Left | N | 2.8 |
| County A | Right | E | 9.3 |
| Hwy 20 | Right | E | 0.4 |

# FOR MORE INFORMATION

**Rustic Road Program**

www.dot.wisconsin.gov/travel/scenic/rusticroads.htm

**Burlington**

Chamber of Commerce 262-763-6044

www.burlingtonchamber.org

ChocolateFest 262-763-3300 www.chocolatefest.com

Spinning Top & Yo-Yo Museum 262-763-3946

www.topmuseum.org

Call for hours

St. Francis Friary & Retreat Center 262-763-3600

**Lyons**

Ye Olde Hotel Bar & Restaurant 262-763-2701

**Lake Geneva**

Chamber of Commerce 800-345-1020 or 262-248-4416

www.lakegenevawi.com

**Racine**

Racine County Convention & Visitor's Bureau 800-272-2463

www.racine.org

Apple Holler Restaurant 262-884-7100 www.appleholler.com

Borzynski's Farm Market 262-886-2235 www.borzynskis.com

Spokes Restaurant & Bar 262-898-7900

**Rochester**

Angel Acres 262-534-7300

Chances Tavern 262-534-2772

Ela Orchard 262-534-2545

Finders Keepers 262-534-9298

Stir Crazy Coffee & Bakery 262-534-1929

**Waterford**

Chamber of Commerce 262-534-5911 www.waterford-wi.org/

Green Meadows Petting Farm 262-534-2891

www.greenmeadowsfarmwi.com

Summer only. Sat. & Sun. Call for hours

Hoppe Homestead Family Dairy Farm 262-534-6480

May–Oct. Call for hours

Uncle Harry's Ice Cream  262-534-4757

Many women I've met have gotten into riding because of a boyfriend or spouse only to find they're scared to death to be "up front." I have this advice for anyone getting into riding:

1) Do it for yourself.
2) Find a motorcycle that fits, not one that someone else wants you to ride. Work with your dealer about ways to shorten the reach and to lower the height of the bike.
3) Take a motorcycle safety course. In Wisconsin, go to the Wisconsin Motorcycle Safety Program website: www.dot.wisconsin.gov/safety/vehicle/motorcyle
4) Remember everyone's at least a little bit scared when they start, but don't let it stop you.
5) Practice, practice, practice. Don't beat yourself up if you make a mistake. And give yourself permission to make only left turns for awhile if right turns make you uncomfortable. When I first started to ride, I avoided a four way stop close to home because it was on a hill. Once I felt more confident, I was ready to try it on my terms and succeeded. Later, I told a friend and his response was, "What hill?"

# 5 BREAKOUT RIDE 2000

Each year in April members of the Kenosha Chapter of the Harley Owners Group® take their Harley-Davidson® motorcycles out of storage. They wash and polish their iron steeds in anticipation of the first chapter ride. So eager are these riders to renew the bonds with their bikes and fellow members that they brave snow, rain, and cold.

The year 2000 was no exception. Over 50 chapter members turned out in 40 degree weather that eventually included rain and sleet. Fortunately, you can choose to ride the same route in 90 degree weather in July.

## NOTES & HIGHLIGHTS

County D west of Rochester

*Breakout Ride 2000* starts from the Brat Stop on Highway 50 just west of Interstate 94. There are several gas stations and restaurants: McDonalds, Subway, Taco Bell, KFC, and Phoenix Family Restaurant, as well as the Brat Stop.

You will ride west past Bong State Recreational Area. This was originally planned to be an airbase in the late 1950s, but was never completed. The remnants of partially built runways are evident in the now established prairie. North of Bong is R-43/ County Road B, the first of two Rustic Roads that pass through woods and agricultural land.

You will continue into Rochester, which is a quaint little town and a favorite for its small shops. West of Rochester is the second Rustic Road, R-2/Maple Road, with its nice curves and views of the Honey Lake Wildlife Area.

Hargraves Road will take your breath away, literally, as the road drops away after each hill. It leads to Valley View Road, which travels one of the area's glacial ridges. This road is not in the best of shape but well worth the bumps for the sweeping view of the surrounding area. As you turn onto Colbo Road, there is an interesting old stone house on the left. The property also contains a very nice old barn. Further down the road in a little valley you might find several donkeys grazing or guarding the sheep. One of these ran off with the lead motorcycles in April 2000 and spawned numerous jokes about the leader.

Donkeys on Colbo Rd.

East Troy is a good place to take a break. The East Troy Electric Railroad Museum on Church Street is just a few blocks off the route as it enters the village square. Built in 1907, the museum is a functioning electric trolley line that makes a ten-mile round trip to the Elegant Farmer outside Mukwonago. The trip takes about an hour. Also on Church Street is Lauber's Old Fashioned Ice Cream parlor, a step back in time for ice cream treats. As you head out of town on County ES, you'll pass Gus's Drive-In. This is a very biker-friendly establishment with good sandwiches and ice cream concoctions.

The second half of *Breakout Ride 2000* includes three roads you won't want to miss. Scotch Bush has some nice tight turns and seems quite secluded. Who could pass up a road with the name of Hodunk? That it has some drop away hills is a bonus. Bowers Road has valleys and curves and a house so close to the road you can nearly touch the owner on the porch.

County D takes you back into Rochester through a curvy tunnel of trees—a colorful ride in the fall. County J winds past Mt. Tom, which was a popular spot for hill climbs in the 1960s and '70s. Many of the old-timers can relate stories of their near-miss exploits.

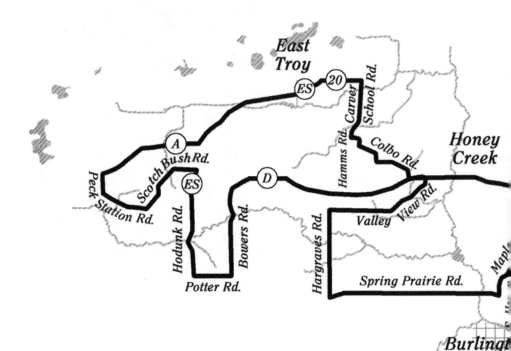

# BREAKOUT RIDE 2000
## 100 MILES

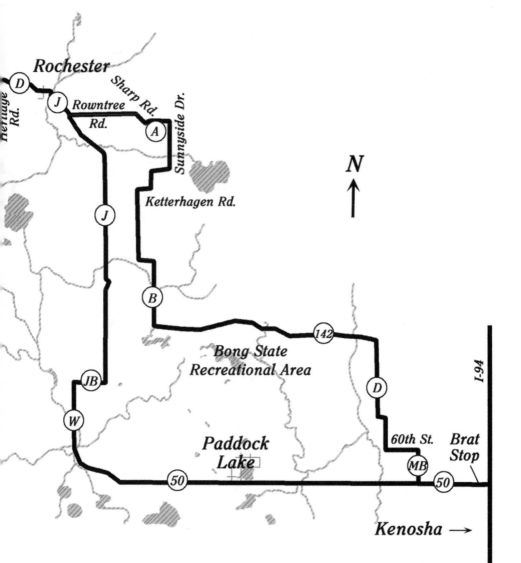

# BREAKOUT RIDE 2000 - 100 MILES

Start west of Kenosha. Leave from the Brat Stop on Hwy 50 just west of I-94.

| Road | Direction | | Miles |
|------|-----------|---|-------|
| Hwy 50 | Right | W | 2.0 |
| County MB | Right | N | 1.0 |
| 60th St. | Left | W | 1.1 |
| County D | Right | N | 1.1 |
| Hwy 142 | Left | W | 3.5 |
| County B | Right | N | 3.7 |
| Sheard Rd. | Straight | N | 1.0 |
| Ketterhagen Rd. | Right | E | 1.4 |
| Sunnyside Dr. | Left | N | 1.5 |
| County A/Plank Rd. | Left | W | 0.7 |
| Sharp Rd. | Right | N | 0.5 |
| Rowntree Rd. | Left | W | 2.0 |
| County J | Right | N | 1.1 |
| County D via Rochester | Left | W | 2.0 |
| Heritage Rd. | Left | S | 1.4 |
| Maple Rd. | Left | S | 1.9 |
| S. Honey Lake Rd. | Left | S | 0.6 |
| Spring Prairie Rd. | Right | W | 5.2 |
| Hargraves Rd. | Right | N | 2.6 |
| Valley View Rd. | Right | E | 3.4 |
| County D | Left | W | 0.5 |
| Colbo Rd. | Right | N | 2.2 |
| Hamms Rd. | Right | N | 0.2 |
| Honey Creek Rd. | Left | W | 0.2 |
| Carver School Rd. | Right | N | 1.9 |
| Hwy 20 | Left | W | 1.1 |
| County ES via East Troy | Left | S | 4.5 |
| County A | Right | W | 3.3 |
| Peck Station Rd. | Left | S | 1.4 |
| Scotch Bush Rd. | Left | E | 2.9 |
| County ES | Right | S | 0.8 |
| County D | Left | E | 0.1 |
| Hodunk Rd. | Right | S | 2.5 |
| Potter Rd. | Left | E | 1.3 |

| Road | Direction | | Miles |
|---|---|---|---|
| Bowers Rd. | Left | N | 2.6 |
| County D via Rochester | Right | E | 11.8 |
| County J | Right | S | 9.6 |
| County JB | Right | W | 1.0 |
| County W | Left | S | 2.5 |
| Hwy 50 | Left | E | 12.6 |

## FOR MORE INFORMATION

**Bong State Recreation Area** (state park sticker required)
262-878-5600
www.dnr.wi.gov/org/land/parks/specific/bong
**Burlington**
Chamber of Commerce 262-763-6044
www.burlingtonchamber.org
ChocolateFest 262-763-3300 www.chocolatefest.com
Spinning Top & Yo-Yo Museum 262-763-3946
www.topmuseum.org
Call for hours
St. Francis Friary & Retreat Center 262-763-3600
**East Troy**
Chamber of Commerce 262-642-3770
www.easttroywi.org
Alpine Valley Music Theatre 262-642-4400
Buell Motorcycle Company 262-642-2020 Call about tours
East Troy Electric Railroad 262-642-3263 Summer only
Elegant Farmer 262-363-6770 www.elegantfarmer.com
Lauber's Old Fashioned Ice Cream Parlor 262-642-3679
Gus's Drive-In 262-642-2929 www.gussdrivein.com
**Kenosha**
Convention & Visitor's Bureau 800-654-7309
www.kenoshacvb.com
Bristol Renaissance Faire 847-395-7773 www.renfair.com/bristol
summer weekends, call for dates

**Kenosha** (cont.)

Jelly Belly Candy Co. 800-522-3267 www.jellybelly.com
Tours daily, exc. major holidays
Russell Military Museum 847-395-7020
www.russellmilitarymuseum.com
Uke's Harley-Davidson/Buell 262-857-8537 www.ukeshd.com

**Rochester**

Angel Acres 262-534-7300
Chances Tavern 262-534-2772
Ela Orchard 262-534-2545
Finders Keepers 262-534-9298
Stir Crazy Coffee & Bakery 262-534-1929

# II - KETTLE MORAINE

**KETTLE MORAINE SCENIC DRIVE - 117 MILES**
**HOLY HILL SIDE TRIP - 23 MILES**

# II - KETTLE MORAINE

The Wisconsin Glacier covered the state 14,000 years ago with a mile-thick sheet of ice. As it advanced and retreated the glacier created end moraines and kettles. Moraines, composed of rock, gravel, and sand, formed as the glacier scraped over the landscape and left this debris in nearly parallel lines. Kettles were formed when the glacier retreated and great chunks of ice were buried in the moraines. As the ice melted, the debris caved in, leaving potholes (kettles).

As the glacier moved over Wisconsin, it separated into six lobes. Two of these lobes were created as the glacier moved south around the uplands of Door County. The Kettle Moraine area was formed when the two lobes began coming together around Plymouth. Because they were both carrying vast amounts of debris, the two lobes bumped and ground against each other as they moved as far south as Janesville. The advance and retreat of the glacier left the parallel lines of moraine for nearly 120 miles.

Some of the moraines were over 300 feet high and can still be seen. Others have been destroyed by erosion and by human activity. Building and mining have been the biggest culprits. In 1936 the Kettle Moraine State Forest was designated to preserve this natural wonder with land purchased from the Izaak Walton League. The league sold the property to the state with the provision that it remain a wildlife preserve.

There are three units in the Kettle Moraine State Forest: Southern, Lapham Peak, and Northern. The Southern unit, in parts of Waukesha, Jefferson, and Walworth Counties, covers 21,000 acres. The Lapham Peak unit, near Delafield, covers 671 acres and is the highest point in Waukesha

Dundee Kame

County at 1,233 feet above sea level. The unit's 45-foot-high observation tower provides a good view of the surrounding features. The Northern unit is in parts of Fond du Lac, Sheboygan, and Washington Counties and covers nearly 30,000 acres. It has its own 60-foot observation tower, Parnell Tower. The Northern unit was the first section designated as the Kettle Moraine State Forest.

All three units have hiking trails and picnic areas. The Southern and Northern units also have camping facilities.

The Northern unit is also a part of the Ice Age National Scientific Reserve, which is a cooperative effort between the State of Wisconsin and the National Park Service. The Henry S. Ruess Ice Age Visitor Center contains exhibits explaining the effects of the ice age on the terrain of Wisconsin. The Ice Age Visitor Center is also part of the Ice Age National Scenic Trail, which attempts to follow the end moraines of the Wisconsin glacier. There are currently 225 miles of trail that are certified by the National Park Service and an additional 250 miles of trail on public and private lands open to public use throughout Wisconsin. When the scenic trail is completed, it will have 1,000 miles of trail.

There are two routes totaling 140 miles in the **Kettle Moraine** section:

- *Kettle Moraine Scenic Drive,* broken up into three maps— southern, middle, and northern
- *Holy Hill Side Trip*

The *Kettle Moraine Scenic Drive* starts in Whitewater and ends in Plymouth. There is not a return route, but I would recommend Highway 67 south. This road goes through parts of the Northern and Southern units and is scenic without all the stops and turns.

The *Holy Hill Side Trip* begins at the junction of County K and Highway 167 (located on the middle map of the *Kettle Moraine Scenic Drive*).

The Kettle Moraine Scenic Drive connects the Northern and Southern Units of the Kettle Moraine State Forest and was laid out to provide a way for visitors to easily enjoy the varied beauty of the glacial landscape. It can be recognized by the acorn shape on the green signs.

Follow this sign

Several years ago two friends and I set out to ride the entire Scenic Drive. We were unaware of any maps featuring the entire route and weren't sure of the actual beginning or end. We knew approximately where it started near Whitewater and set out from there to follow the signs. The drive is well marked within the state forest units, but not outside state property. We were continually frustrated by signs that were nonexistent, weatherworn, or facing the wrong way. There are also no signs announcing the beginning or the end of the drive. From that initial ride, it was my mission to map the entire Kettle Moraine Scenic Drive. Since publication of *Sunday Rides*, the DNR has issued a handout with driving instructions but no maps. It is available at all Kettle Moraine State Forest offices or online.

Because of the length, I have divided the Scenic Drive into three maps with the directions at the end. The route is also lengthy in time because of the slow speeds and curvy roads on much of the route. Remember, the return is also 117 miles!

## NOTES & HIGHLIGHTS

The route begins in Whitewater, although the Scenic Drive actually begins about five miles south of the city. Whitewater is home to the University of Wisconsin–Whitewater and has all the accoutrements of a small college town. My favorite restaurant for breakfast is Jessica's on Main Street.

You will start to see the "Acorn" signs on Kettle Moraine Drive. (Note: there are many roads along the Scenic Drive that use this same name. Nearly all of them are scenic and offer some fine riding.) This is one of my favorites in the Southern unit, as it winds by Whitewater Lake and Rice Lake under a canopy of trees. The curves begin to widen out on County H as you head by the John Muir Hiking and Bicycling Trails. Just a mile or so back is the quaint La Grange General Store, which has a unique sandwich menu along with holistic foods and herbals as well as bicycle rentals and supplies. You will often see lycra and leather mixing on the front porch.

Both the towns of Palmyra and Eagle offer restaurants and gas stations. Just south of Eagle on Hwy 67 is Old World Wisconsin which features many original settlers' homes and buildings on 800 acres. There are many events throughout the year where volunteers reenact the lives of the buildings' occupants.

County ZZ and Town G both offer tight curves with lots of shade against the heat of a July day. And if you need a break from riding along County C, stop at the Lapham Peak Unit and climb the steps of the observation tower. Increase A. Lapham was the father of the National Weather Service, approved in 1870. One of the original signal stations was erected on Lapham Peak.

Delafield has restaurants and shopping galore. It's the home of the Lang Companies, and there are several shops at which to buy the notepads, calendars, candles, and boxes that have made them successful.

A short drive west of County C on Wells Street is the Hawks Inn. This is a completely renovated 1846 stage stop with period furnishings. Seventeen of the 22 rooms are open to the public.

St. John's Northwestern Military Academy is also in

St. John's Military Academy

St. John's Military Academy

Delafield and is open to ride through. The architecture is unusual for the area and definitely militaristic.

West on Mission Avenue on the outskirts of Delafield is Nashotah House, an Episcopal seminary founded in 1842. It is the oldest institution granting degrees in Wisconsin. The grounds are open to the public.

The ride gets more interesting from Nashotah to North Lake as it winds along several lakes lined with expensive homes and some beautiful landscaping. In the mid-1800s this area became the summer playground for wealthy Milwaukee businessmen and their families. In 1884 Frederick Pabst purchased the Nashotah Inn, which had been built in 1848 as a stage stop. He renamed it Red Circle Inn, and it is now the oldest continuing restaurant in Wisconsin.

Once you cross into Washington County on County K, begin to look ahead to your right, and Holy Hill will appear like magic in the distance. It's one of the most striking landmarks featured in this book. You can take the Holy Hill Side Trip to get up close and personal.

One of the highest points in the region is located in Pike Lake State Park. Powder Kame is 1,350 feet above sea level. The Ice Age National Scenic Trail passes through the park.

The northern portion of the Scenic Drive is my favorite because the glacial landscape seems more rugged and untamed. Beginning with Kettle Moraine Drive north of West Bend, the route soars along glacial ridges, twists and turns through pine forests, and glides through meadows. My favorite road is Kettle Moraine Drive just south of Greenbush; it will hone your skills in the tight, hilly turns. The Greenbush Kettle is also found along this road.

The Ice Age Visitor Center has extensive exhibits and information about the glaciers. Helpful rangers will answer your questions. Fuel up in Slinger or Dundee because there is nothing in between. There are good hamburgers and ice cream in Dundee. Stop to stretch your legs at the Parnell Tower, which is located on County U a quarter mile west of County A.

The 60-foot-tall observation tower will afford you a view of the area for miles and miles.

Wade House, a restored 1851 stagecoach inn and carriage museum in

Parnell Tower

Greenbush, is one of several historical sites renovated by the State Historical Society. A new feature of Wade House is the Herrling Sawmill, an authentic replica of the original waterpowered sawmill that stood on the Mullet River from 1854 to 1910. There are many reenactment events held there, including a Civil War encampment in the fall.

The Scenic Drive ends at the Sheboygan Marsh. In Elkhart Lake you will find, among other lodging and activities, the Siebkens Resort (a turn-of-the-century resort on Elkhart Lake), the Osthoff Resort (a swanky four diamond hotel), and Road America (a road racing venue for Indy cars and motorcycles). Keep your eyes open for a Paul Newman sighting.

If you don't want to retrace your steps back to Whitewater, an easy alternative route is Highway 67, which you will find just to the east of Elkhart Lake by following County A.

When it's cold I wear a heated jacket and gloves with a thermostat that keeps me at a constant temperature. After riding hours with the thermosat exposed to the rain, I found out that it wasn't waterproof. Little curls of smoke and an odd smell convinced me it was time to turn it off. I cover the new one with a baggy.

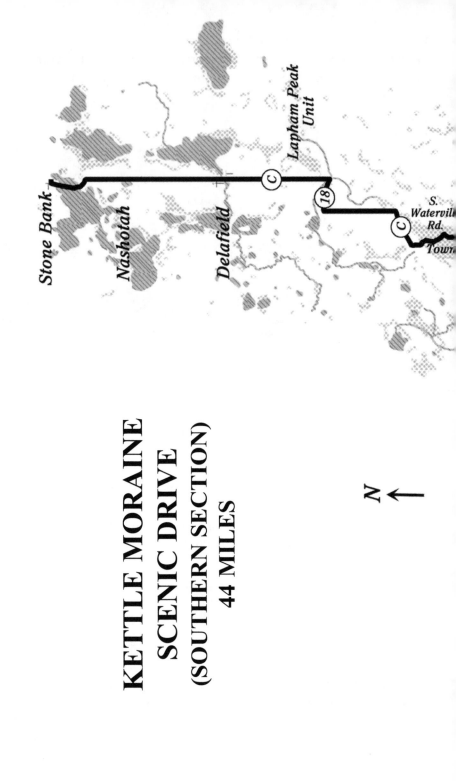

# KETTLE MORAINE
## SCENIC DRIVE
### (SOUTHERN SECTION)
#### 44 MILES

N

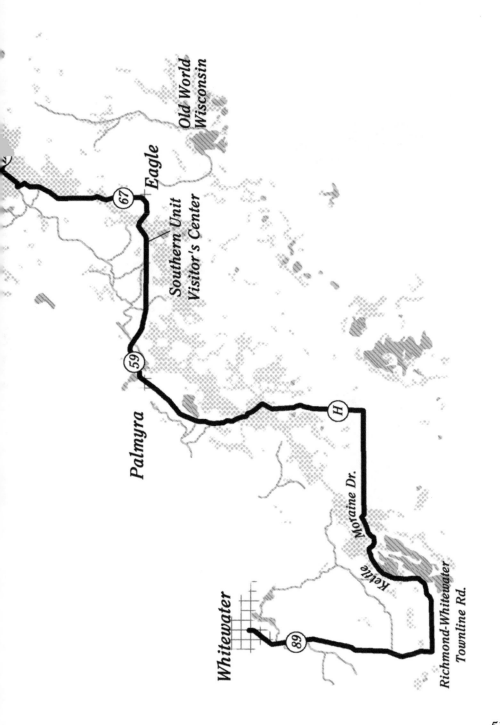

Old World
Wisconsin

Eagle

67

Southern Unit
Visitor's Center

59

Palmyra

H

Moraine Dr.

Kettle

Richmond-Whitewater
Townline Rd.

Whitewater

89

# KETTLE MORAINE
# SCENIC DRIVE
## (MIDDLE SECTION)
## 39 MILES

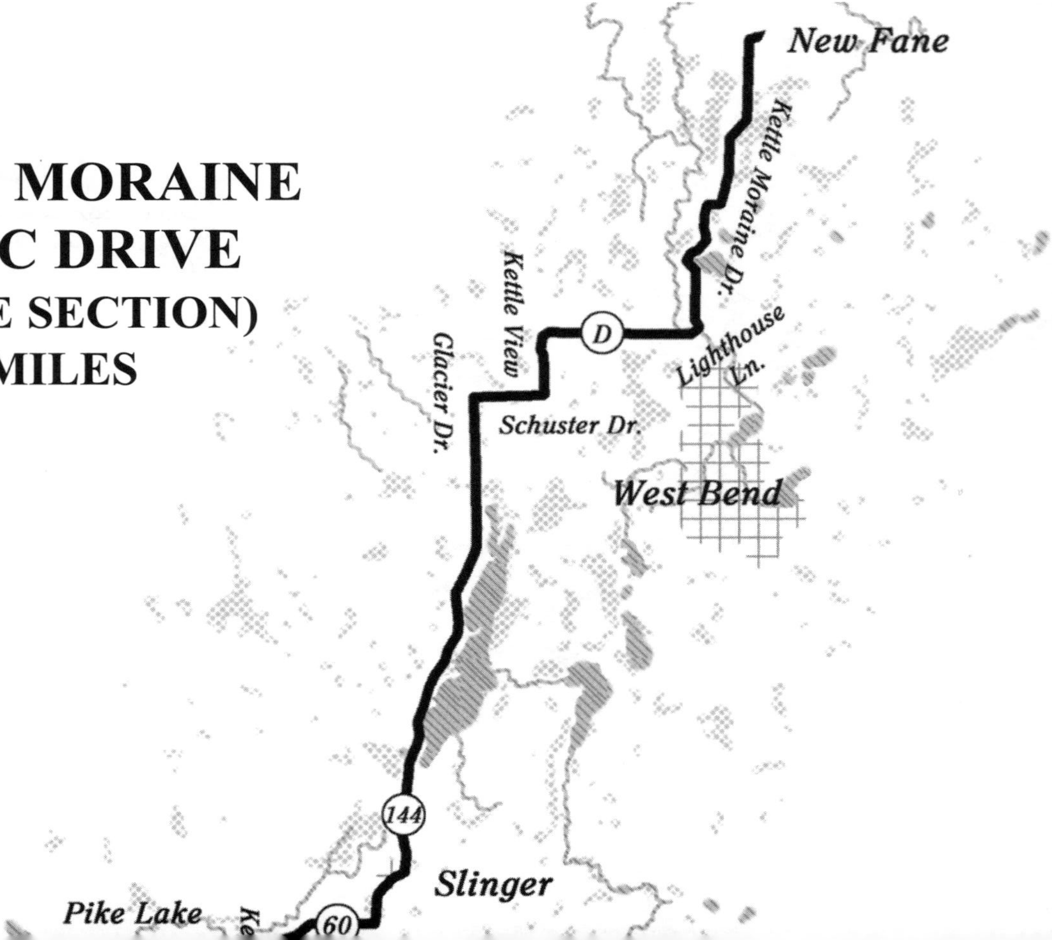

New Fane

Kettle Moraine Dr.

Lighthouse

West Bend

D

Schuster Dr.

Kettle View

Glacier Dr.

Slinger

144

60

Ke

Pike Lake

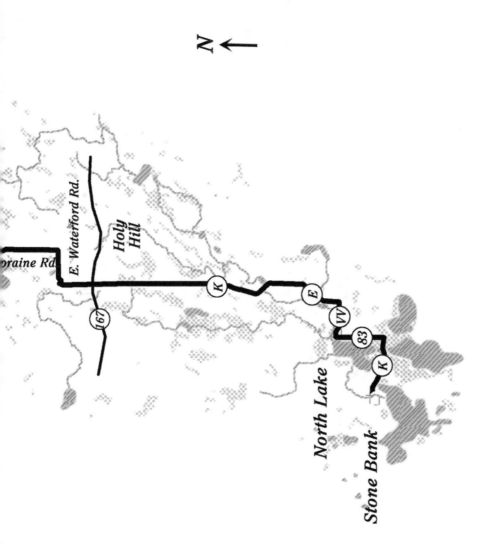

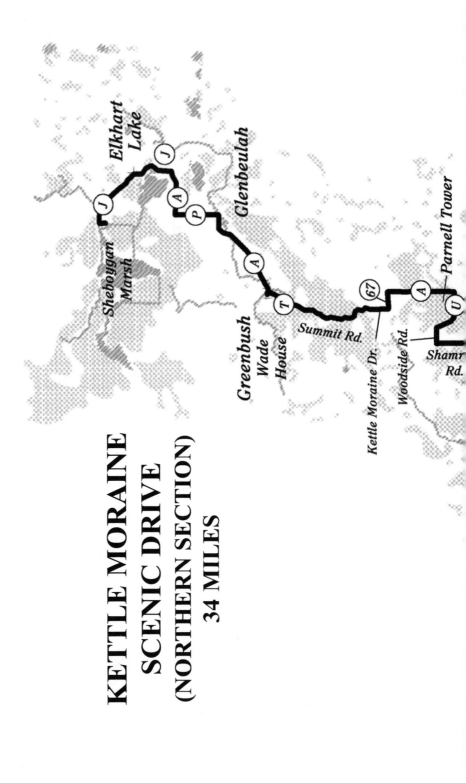

# KETTLE MORAINE SCENIC DRIVE
## (NORTHERN SECTION)
### 34 MILES

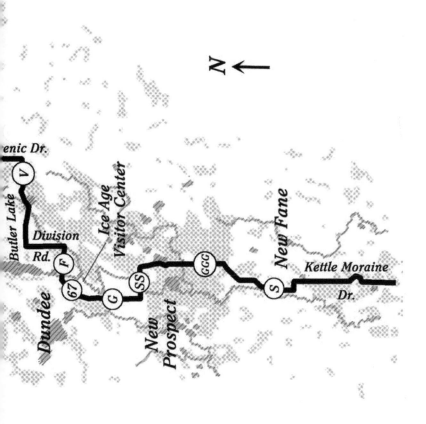

# KETTLE MORAINE SCENIC DRIVE - 117 MILES

Start the tour in Whitewater by going south 5.0 miles on Hwy 89. Turn right on Richmond-Whitewater Townline Road. (There is a house on the southwest corner.) This turns into Kettle Moraine Drive.

| Road | Direction | | Miles |
|------|-----------|---|-------|

**Southern Section**

| Road | Direction | | Miles |
|------|-----------|---|-------|
| Kettle Moraine Dr. | | E | 4.0 |
| County H through Palmyra | Left | N | 7.0 |
| Hwy 59 via Eagle | Straight | E | 6.0 |
| | Visitor's Center on right, 3 miles from Eagle | | |
| Hwy 67 | Left | N | 4.0 |
| County ZZ | Right | E | 2.0 |
| S. Waterville Rd./Town G | Left | N | 2.7 |
| County C through Delafield, Nashotah, & Stone Bank | Right | N | 13.3 |
| | Turn Right on Hwy 18 and left again on County C | | |

**Middle Section** (begins at Stone Bank)

| Road | Direction | | Miles |
|------|-----------|---|-------|
| County K | Right | E | 1.7 |
| Hwy 83 via North Lake | Left | N | 1.5 |
| County VV | Right | E | 1.0 |
| County E | Left | N | 2.9 |
| | Bad railroad crossing on E | | |
| County K | Straight | N | 6.0 |
| E. Waterford Rd. | Right | E | 1.0 |
| | Comes up fast 2.0 miles from 167 | | |
| Kettle Moraine Rd. | Left | N | 2.7 |
| | Pike Lake S.P. | | |
| Hwy 60 | Right | E | 1.6 |
| Hwy 144 via Slinger | Left | N | 7.6 |
| Glacier Dr. | Straight | N | 1.4 |
| Schuster Dr. | Right | E | 1.0 |
| Kettle View | Left | N | 1.0 |
| | Looks like the entrance to a gravel pit | | |
| County D | Right | E | 2.1 |

| | | | |
|---|---|---|---|
| Lighthouse Ln. | Left | N | 0.4 |
| Kettle Moraine Dr. | Left | N | 7.4 |
| | Just overbridge | | |

**Northern Section** (begins at New Fane)

| | | | |
|---|---|---|---|
| County S | Right | N | 2.4 |
| County GGG | Left | N | 2.4 |
| County SS | Left | W | 1.0 |
| County G | Right | N | 2.1 |
| | Ice Age Visitor Center, turn left onto Hwy 67 for 0.2 miles, center is on left | | |
| Hwy 67 via Dundee | Right | E | 0.3 |
| County F | Straight | E | 1.0 |
| Division Rd. | Left | N | 1.1 |
| Butler Lake Rd. | Right | E | 1.4 |
| County V | Right | E | 1.0 |
| Scenic Dr. | Left | N | 2.0 |
| Shamrock Rd. | Right | N | 1.1 |
| Woodside Rd. | Right | E | 0.4 |
| County U | Right | S | 1.4 |
| | Parnell   Tower | | |
| County U/A | Left | N | 3.0 |
| Hwy 67 | Left | W | 0.5 |
| Kettle Moraine Dr. | Right | N | 1.3 |
| Summit Rd. | Left | N | 2.3 |
| County T | Right | N | 0.4 |
| Washington St. | Left | W | 0.1 |
| Center St. | Right | N | 0.2 |
| | Past WadeHouse | | |
| County T/A via Greenbush | Right/Left | E/N | 2.7 |
| County A/P via Glenbeulah | Left | N | 1.2 |
| County A | Right | E | 1.3 |
| County J via Elkhart Lake | Left | N | 0.4 |
| Osthoff Ave. | Left | W | .9 |
| Rhine St. | Left | W | .2 |
| County J | Right | N | 1.9 |

Ends at Sheboygan Marsh

# 2 HOLY HILL SIDE TRIP

Sooner or later every motorcyclist in southern Wisconsin makes it up the winding road to Holy Hill, the National Shrine of Mary as it is known formally. Or, at least it seems like every

Holy Hill from County K

motorcycle is there on a warm fall day.

The shrine is an imposing structure with towering spires and beautiful stained glass windows. But it wasn't always so. Holy Hill started as a wooden cross erected by a town of Erin resident in 1855.

Emerald Rd.

When a local hermit was miraculously cured, it became a place of pilgrimage. To accommodate an increasing number of worshipers, the current building was erected in 1931. The original wooden cross can be seen outside the main doors of the church. Currently the shrine is overseen by the Roman Catholic Discalced Carmelite Order of Friars.

Regular worship services are held, and there is a half-mile outdoor Stations of the Cross with beautiful statuary depicting Christ's journey. The church and grounds are open to the public. Donations are always welcome.

## NOTES & HIGHLIGHTS

The setting of the church is breathtaking, even more so after a climb up the 178 steps to the observation platform in one of the spires. The view of the southern Kettle Moraine is truly a magnificent sight.

When your thighs stop screaming, take a walk to the cafeteria for soups, sandwiches, desserts, and refreshing drinks. There are even baked goods to take home. If you're up to it, wander the 400 acres around the church. The Ice Age Trail goes through the property.

Once you're back on the motorcycle, ride the many Rustic Roads around Holy Hill between County K and Q. They are all numbered R-33, and this route forms a loop. St. Augustine Road is filled with tight curves and swooping hills. You may get a glimpse of Lowe Lake off Emerald Road through the many trees that line the road and form a canopy. Donegal Road opens up a bit and surprises you with a closer view of Holy Hill. When I rode this route for the first time, I was totally amazed at how much fun the road was and how scenic it was. I couldn't believe this was in Wisconsin. My awe has continued with each subsequent ride through the area.

Spire of church

# HOLY HILL SIDE TRIP
## 23 MILES

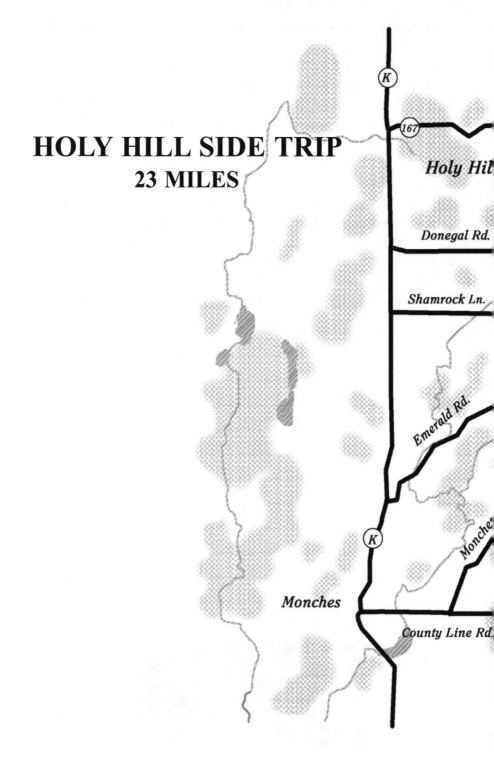

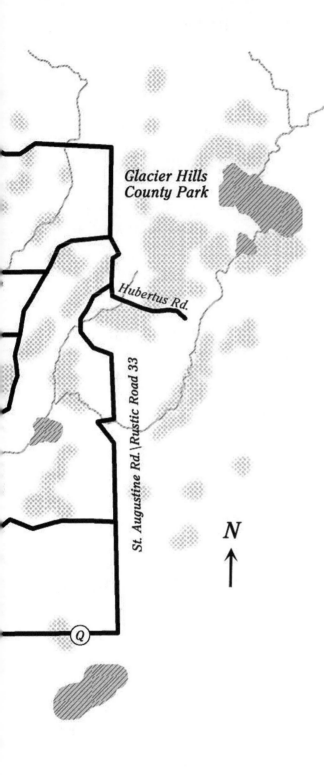

Glacier Hills
County Park

Hubertus Rd.

St. Augustine Rd. \ Rustic Road 33

N

Q

# HOLY HILL SIDE TRIP - 23 MILES

From the Kettle Moraine Scenic Drive, begin the side trip at the corner of County K and Hwy 167.

| Road | Direction | | Miles |
|------|-----------|---|-------|
| Hwy 167 | Right | E | 0.6 |
| Holy Hill entrance road | Right | S | 0.3 |
| Holy Hill | | | |
| Hwy 167 | Right | E | 1.5 |
| St. Augustine Rd./R-33 | Right | S | 5.5 |
| Veer right at first stopsign. No street sign. Cont. on St. Augustine Rd. | | | |
| County Line Rd./County Q | Right | W | 1.6 |
| Monches Rd. | Right | N | 2.1 |
| St. Augustine Rd. | Left | N | 2.5 |
| Emerald Rd. | Left | S | 3.4 |
| County K | Right | N | 1.4 |
| Shamrock Ln. | Right | E | 1.2 |
| Emerald Rd. | Left | N | 0.5 |
| Donegal Rd. | Left | W | 1.4 |
| County K | Right | N | 0.9 |

People ask me if I'm afraid for my safety when I travel, and I can honestly say I'm not. I believe there are three keys to traveling safely:

1) **Plan.** Know where you're going and where you're going to stay.

2) **Attitude.** Walk, talk, & ride with confidence (or at least fake it).

3) **Listen to your inner voice.** There's no need to look for bogey men, but if something doesn't seem quite right, it probably isn't.

# FOR MORE INFORMATION

**Delafield**

Chamber of Commerce 262-646-8100
www.delafield-wi.org
Hawks Inn 262-646-4794 www.hawksinn.org
May–October, fee
St. John's Northwestern Military Academy 800-752-2338
www.sjnma.org

**Eagle**

Old World Wisconsin 262-594-6300
www.oldworldwisconsin.org
May–October, fee

**Elkhart Lake**

Tourism Office 877-355-4278 www.elkhartlake.com
Osthoff Resort 800-876-3399 www.osthoff.com
Road America 800-365-7223 www.roadamerica.com
Siebkens Resort 920-876-2600 www.siebkens.com

**Greenbush**

Wade House & Herrling Sawmill 920-526-3271
www.wadehouse.org
May–October, fee

**Holy Hill** 262-628-1838 www.holyhill.com

**Kettle Moraine State Forest** (state park sticker required)
www.dnr.wi.gov/org/land/parks/specific/kmscenicdrive/
Southern Unit 262-594-6200
Lapham Peak Unit 262-646-3025
Northern Unit & Ice Age Visitor Center 262-626-2116
Pike Lake Unit 262-670-3400

**Nashotah**

Village Clerk 262 367-8440
Nashotah House 262-646-3371
Red Circle Inn 262-367-4883 or 262-367-7888

**Whitewater**

Chamber of Commerce 262-473-4005
www.whitewaterchamber.com

# III - DRIFTLESS AREA

# III - DRIFTLESS AREA

The Wisconsin Glacier of 14,000 years ago was the major force forming the terrain in most of Wisconsin except the southwest portion. The unglaciated portion of the state became known as the Driftless

Stable on County H

Area or the Uplands. The transition area between the two landscapes runs through the northeast portion of Green County and the southwest portion of Dane County. A 22-mile section of the Ice Age National Scenic Trail that follows the end moraines can be found along the Sugar River Recreational Trail. The Driftless Area appears substantially different from the rest of Wisconsin and is marked by long winding ridges, steep valleys, and many twisting streams and rivers.

Southwest Wisconsin attracted many settlers searching for the familiarity of their homeland. Early immigrants in the 1830s were the hard-rock miners of Cornwall, England, who came to the area after lead was discovered. Later, in the 1840s, pioneers from Switzerland were attracted to the New Glarus area, and Norwegians came to Mt. Horeb, Blue Mound, and settlements north of the Wisconsin River. Their influence is still seen in the Uplands today.

Lead and zinc mining played a large part in the area's history beginning in the 1820s. Wisconsin's nickname "Badgers" came from the description of the miners as they dug into the hills like badgers. Southwest Wisconsin had such economic importance that it claimed the seat of the Wisconsin territory in two places—Belmont for 46 days in 1836 and Mineral Point from 1836 to 1848. For a brief time this section of the state was the major mining center in the world. Eventually the ore declined and the gold in California beckoned. On one day in 1849, sixty wagons left Mineral Point for California. The area had a resurgence of mining in the 1870s when zinc was found in the lead tailings. This industry began to die out after World War I, although the last zinc mine didn't close until 1979.

Many of the old and new settlers turned to dairy farming and cheesemaking. The advent of refrigerated railroad cars increased the cheese market, and in the early 1890s there were 30 cheesemaking companies within 30 miles of Blanchardville. Today there are still over a dozen cheese factories in Green County helping to make Wisconsin the number one cheese producer in the country. The Historic Cheesemaking Center in Monroe showcases the history of the industry and its influence on the area.

Dairy farms and Holstein cows (the black and white ones) are prominent in southwestern Wisconsin, where the family farm still predominates. The Breakfast on the Farm program was started by one of these families in Green County in 1979. Since then it has spread to other counties, and the public is invited to participating dairy farms for a traditional breakfast of eggs, cheese, and sausage.

The Driftless Area is one of my favorite places to ride. It's known for its long ridges and deep valleys. Roads swoop up and around and twist and turn. At one point you will be racing along looking over the surrounding farmland and feeling on top of the world. Next you are plunging down into a cool valley with a trout stream on one side and a rock face on the other. It seems there's a surprise hidden around every turn and beyond every hill.

There are five routes totaling 507 miles in the **Driftless Area**:

- *Hidden Valleys*
- *Ridge Runner*
- *America's Dairyland*
- *Badger Country*
- *Galena Circle*

Except for *Galena Circle,* all the routes start in New Glarus, "America's Little Switzerland." *Galena Circle* begins in the Illinois town of Galena. Most of the roads are in good shape, lightly traveled, and narrow.

*Hidden Valleys* starts off in New Glarus, where you could spend at least a day sightseeing or shopping. If you're anxious to get on the bike

Miles of curves

and ride, you'll be rewarded, as this route exemplifies the Uplands with its long ridges, steep valleys, and winding roads. Full sun shines warmly on the hilltops and is nearly blocked out by the trees and rock walls in the valleys.

Rural character abounds in finely kept white farmhouses, dairy cows on the hillsides, and fields flowing with the contours of the land. Rural smells are also evident in the sweetness of fermenting livestock feed and the pungency of manure. As you know, one of the benefits of motorcycling is getting the full experience.

## NOTES & HIGHLIGHTS

County H is a good entry to *Hidden Valleys* as it sweeps up and down through a wide valley that narrows in places to tight curves. Postville Road forms the main intersection with County H in Postville, which consists of a few houses and the town hall. It veers off to the left and becomes Dougherty Creek Road.

This road is hilly and twisting and dappled in shadows. It follows a trout stream on one side and a rock face on the other. I encountered three deer here in midday, one standing smack in the middle of the road and one on either side.

After riding up and down one last hill, Dougherty Creek Road spits you out at the blind intersection of Prairie View Road. It is indeed a pleasant view of a house in the valley below and a farm on the far ridge.

Puddledock is a curious name for another wonderful twisting road, with trees on the ridge top and farmland sloping into the valley. Farm buildings are nestled into the landscape.

Holsteins

A road named Rat Hollow demands to be ridden. It's a mild road with a bit of marshland, which in this well drained region is unusual. Also unusual are the road signs: they are small, hand-lettered brown boards that may or may not be lettered on both sides. (Didn't see any rats, though.)

After riding the tight curves, County Roads M and Y allow you to open the throttle into Woodford where Black Hawk County Park is a relaxing spot along the Pecatonica River. Highway 78 continues off the route into Argyle, where there are places for gas and food. Argyle is the gateway to Yellowstone Lake State Park and home to the Argyle Power Plant. At one time power was generated on the rivers throughout the area, but this is one of the few remaining in southwest Wisconsin.

Heading west on Highway 81 will put you back on the route toward Old Q Road. This roller coaster of hills might get you off your seat. At the top the view stretches for miles and miles. It is one of several roads that allows you to "Ride the Ridges" into Blanchardville. The little community founded in 1847 is very proud of its historic renovations.

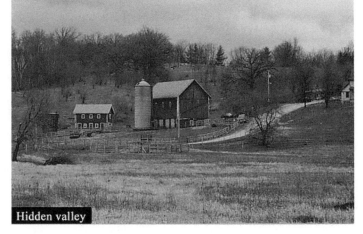
Hidden valley

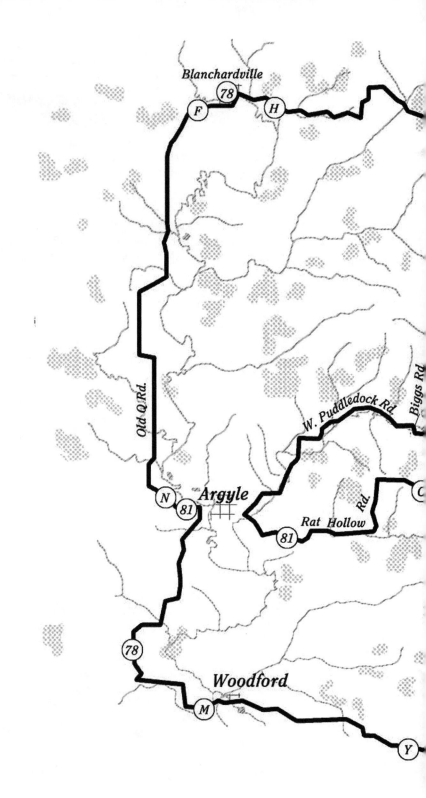

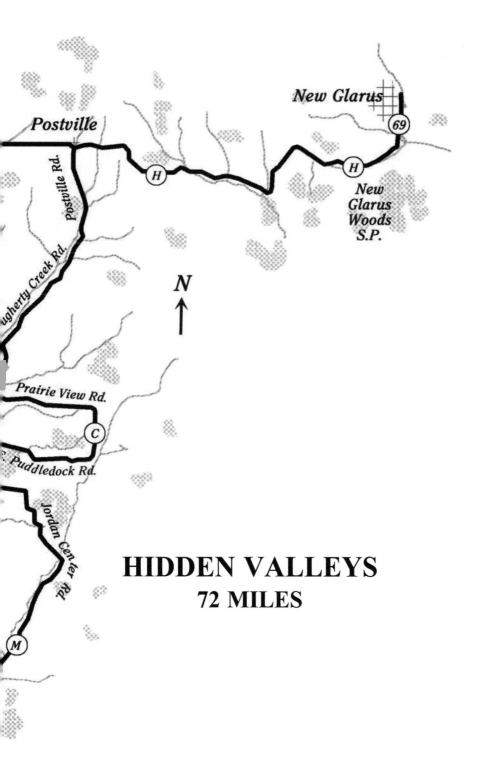

# HIDDEN VALLEYS
## 72 MILES

# HIDDEN VALLEYS - 72 MILES

Start in New Glarus.

| Road | Direction | | Miles |
|------|-----------|---|-------|
| Hwy 69 | | S | 1.1 |
| County H | Right | W | 7.4 |
| Postville Rd. | Left | S | 1.7 |
| Dougherty Creek Rd. | Straight | S | 3.7 |
| Prairie View Rd. | Left | E | 2.4 |
| County C | Right | S | 0.1 |
| E. Puddledock Rd. | Right | W | 3.2 |
| Biggs Rd. | Right | N | 0.1 |
| W. Puddledock Rd. | Left | W | 4.7 |
| Hwy 81 | Left | S | 1.4 |
| Rat Hollow Rd. | Left | N | 2.4 |
| | Small wooden street sign. Just past Green Co. sign | | |
| County C | Right | E | 2.1 |
| Jordan Center Rd. | Right | S | 3.9 |
| | Second right | | |
| | Small wooden street sign facing the opposite way. Make 2 right turns—watch street signs | | |
| County M | Straight | S | 1.8 |
| County Y | Right | W | 4.4 |
| County M | Straight | W | 2.2 |
| Hwy 78 | Right | N | 4.2 |
| Hwy 81 | Left | W | 0.5 |
| County G/County N | Right | N | 1.7 |
| Old Q Rd. | Straight | N | 6.5 |
| County F | Right | E | 0.9 |
| Hwy 78 | Left | N | 0.4 |
| County H | Right | E | 13.7 |
| Hwy 69 | Left | N | 1.1 |

# FOR MORE INFORMATION

**Argyle**
      608-543-3113 www.argylewi.org

**Blanchardville**
      608-523-2274 www.blanchardville.com

**New Glarus**
  Chamber of Commerce 800-527-6838 www.swisstown.com
  Green County Welcome Center 888-222-9111
      www.greencounty.org
  Chalet of the Golden Fleece 800-527-6838
      May–October, fee
  New Glarus Bakery 866-805-5536 www.newglarusbakery.com
  New Glarus Brewing Company 608-527-5850
      www.newglarusbrewing.com
  Ruef's Meat Market 608-527-2554 www.ruefsmeatmarket.com
  Swiss Historical Village 608-527-2317
      www.swisshistoricalvillage.org
      May–October, fee

**New Glarus Woods State Park** (state park sticker required)
      608-527-2335
      www.dnr.wi.gov/org/land/parks/specific/ngwoods

---

The farms and grazing cows make Wisconsin a scenic place. They can also make it a messy one, especially in the spring. All the manure generated by those animals has to go someplace, and what better place than on the fields as fertilizer. Unfortunately, the manure wagons sometimes leak and the fields and roads may be wet. This makes for quite a mix on the roads and on the motorcycle and pants. One particular ride I led was dubbed the "manure ride" after we rode through about a mile of the stuff. Washing the bikes and clothes was not pleasant duty.

Got milk?

Nowhere is the family farm more apparent than on *America's Dairyland*. There are blue silos, red barns, white houses, and black and white cows seemingly around every curve and tucked into every valley.

There are wide open valleys with big loopy curves and narrow ones with tight twists. The tight twists are accompanied by steep hills. I've often wondered how the milk trucks or school buses make it through. This is probably the most challenging route in the book, and unless you want to double the challenge, I recommend not riding this in the early spring. Instead of salting icy winter roads, the rural areas use sand. The left over sand makes cornering slippery, and stopping at the sloping intersections is dicey.

It's almost a relief to get to wide open road where you'll find whooping, roller coaster hills. The views before heading down are breathtaking, too.

You can't help notice the many birdhouses on poles at intervals along the roads. These are part of the efforts of the North American Bluebird Society located in nearby Darlington to increase the bluebirds' nesting habitat. If you dare to do the route in spring, you will probably see one or two as they return to the area.

## NOTES & HIGHLIGHTS

County Roads O and U are in the transition area between the Driftless and Glacial regions. The valleys are broader and flatter and the curves are fast and fun leading to Paoli.

Like many small towns in the Driftless Area, Paoli is enjoying a renaissance. Artists and craftspeople have been attracted to the beauty of the older buildings and the lower rents. There are several shops and galleries in Paoli with interesting and unusual items.

Paoli

Head out of Paoli on Range Trail and leave the wide valleys behind. The road here seems to hang between the ridge and the valley and is topped with branches.

The route takes you just south of Verona, but if you stay on County M you will find gas stations and restaurants. The next gas station is 33 miles away in Hollandale.

The serious riding begins on Spring Rose Road, heads onto Britt Valley Road, which runs narrowly between a rock face and a twisting stream, and continues on Perry Center Road by adding some steep curves. County Roads A and DD are where you'll find the breathtaking views.

Lake Road rolls into Yellowstone Lake State Park, home of the largest lake in southwest Wisconsin. This planned lake was made by damming the Yellowstone River. You might see one of several eagles that reside in the area, as well as a variety of waterfowl.

County C lies atop a long winding ridge and flows easily even with a little more throttle. County N is the main roller coaster event on this route.

Bluebird house

# AMERICA'S DAIRYLAND
## 100 MILES

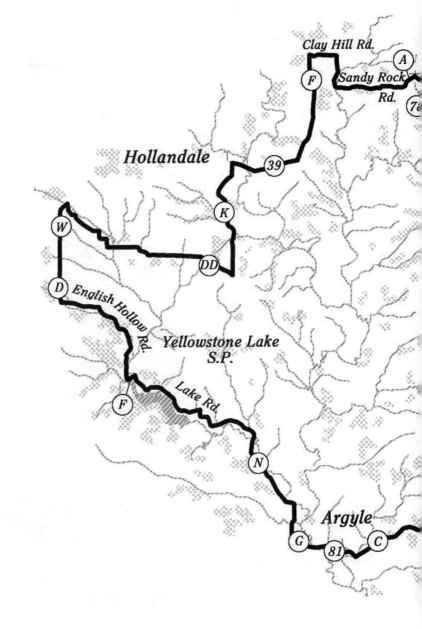

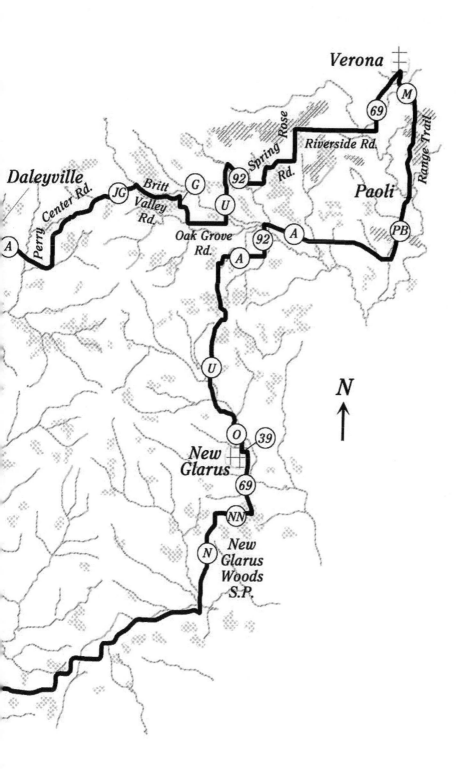

# AMERICA'S DAIRYLAND - 100 MILES

Start in New Glarus.

| Road | Direction | | Miles |
|------|-----------|---|-------|
| Hwy 39 | | W | 0.3 |
| County O | Right | N | 2.4 |
| County U | Right | N | 4.4 |
| County A | Right | E | 1.3 |
| Hwy 92 | Left | N | 1.0 |
| County A | Right | E | 4.5 |
| County PB via Paoli | Left | N | 2.2 |
| Range Trail | Left | N | 3.0 |
| Just before "downtown" | | | |
| County M via Verona | Left | N | 1.0 |
| Paoli St./Hwy 69 | Left | S | 2.1 |
| No sign for Hwy 69/left turn lane | | | |
| Riverside Rd. | Right | W | 2.7 |
| Just before curve/school forest sign | | | |
| Spring Rose Rd. | Left | S | 2.6 |
| Hwy 92 | Right | W | 1.4 |
| County U | Left | S | 1.9 |
| Oak Grove Rd. | Right | W | 2.0 |
| County G | Right | N | 0.3 |
| Britt Valley Rd. | Left | W | 1.6 |
| County JG | Left | W | 1.0 |
| Perry Center Rd. | Right | S | 3.5 |
| At Spring Valley, go right then left | | | |
| County A | Right | W | 2.8 |
| Hwy 78 | Right | N | 0.6 |
| County A | Left | W | 0.4 |
| Sandy Rock Rd. | Right | W | 3.1 |
| Midway, continue straight at intersection | | | |
| Clay Hill Rd. | Left | N | 1.1 |
| County F | Left | S | 3.4 |

| Road | Direction | | Miles |
|---|---|---|---|
| Hwy 39 | Right | W | 2.3 |
| County K | Left | S | 3.8 |
| County DD | Right | W | 7.4 |
| County W | Left | S | 3.1 |
| County D | Straight | S | 0.1 |
| English Hollow Rd. | Left | E | 3.9 |
| | Comes up fast after Co. D sign | | |
| County F | Left | N | 0.3 |
| Lake Rd. through S.P. | Right | E | 5.3 |
| | Exit S.P., stay on Lake Rd. | | |
| County N | Right | S | 3.7 |
| County G | Left | E | 0.6 |
| Hwy 81 via Argyle | Left | E | 1.6 |
| County C | Left | E | 11.3 |
| County N | Left | N | 3.1 |
| County NN | Right | E | 1.3 |
| Hwy 69 | Left | N | 1.9 |

# FOR MORE INFORMATION

**New Glarus**
See page 73
**Paoli**
Artisan Gallery 608-845-6600 www.artisangal.com/about.lasso
closed Monday
January & February open Sat. & Sun. only
**Verona**
Chamber of Commerce 608-845-5777
www.veronawi.com
**Yellowstone Lake State Park** (state park sticker required)
608-523-4427
www.dnr.wi.gov/org/land/parks/specific/yellowstone

# 3  RIDGE RUNNER

*Ridge Runner* follows mostly county highways, but they are such scenic and lightly traveled roads it's hard not to use them. *Ridge Runner*

Shed on County U

runs generally along the valleys and over the ridges, which makes for steep hills and wide curves. I'm always impressed with how green the valleys are, with their woodlots and tree-covered slopes.

The route makes a small loop through Monticello and back up to New Glarus for the continuation of the ride. You may be tempted to skip this part but you will miss some very nice scenery.

## NOTES & HIGHLIGHTS

*Ridge Runner* begins in New Glarus, "America's Little Switzerland," founded in 1845 by 108 Swiss from the Canton of Glarus. Continued immigration and familial ties have kept the German/Swiss heritage alive, and it is celebrated at three annual festivals: the Heidi Festival in June, Volkfest (Swiss Independence Day) on the first Sunday in August, and the Wilhelm Tell Festival (a drama of Swiss independence) in September. You can learn more about the heritage and settlers at the fourteen replica buildings in the Swiss Historical Village.

Monticello is one of the friendliest small towns; even the whimsical windsocks and flags on the utility poles welcome you. Stop at the M & M Cafe for breakfast or lunch and say "hi" to Mike and Mary. Or enjoy a leisurely walk over the footbridge to the island in Lake Montesian.

Marshall Bluff and Tunnel Roads follow the valley floor and curve under the tree branches and around rock walls. Tunnel Road gets its name because a tunnel was built through the rock to accomodate the railroad. The rails have since been dug up for a bicycle trail, but the tunnel can be found a short walk off the road.

Traffic picks up a bit back on Highway 69 as you complete the loop to New Glarus. County O connecting with County G has nice easy curves and hills to lead you into Mt. Vernon. This picturesque small town invites you to stay.

While researching *Ridge Runner*, I became so caught up with the beauty and fun of riding Highway 92, it took me eight miles before I realized I'd missed my turn. I've included some of those eight miles.

The Norwegian community of Mt. Horeb is one of the several ethnic settlements in southwest Wisconsin and is known as the troll capital of the world. Legend has it that trolls buried and now guard the earth's last remaining precious stones and minerals. Maps are available to help you locate the 18 trolls that lurk in and around Mt. Horeb. Hint: most of them are on the Trollway (Main Street). There's also good eats and shopping.

Troll - Mt. Horeb

If searching for trolls isn't hard enough for you, Blue Mound State Park has two 40-foot observation towers you can climb to view the area. At 1,719 feet, this is the highest spot in southern Wisconsin. The park gets its name because the mound looks blue from a distance.

Highway 78 is a reason in itself to take this route. I love the wide sweeping curves of it. This is one of those great roads that makes you want to keep motorcycling forever. And it just keeps getting better as you turn onto County Road A for some roller coaster hills. Highway 39 combines easy curves with panoramic views as you fly along the ridge top.

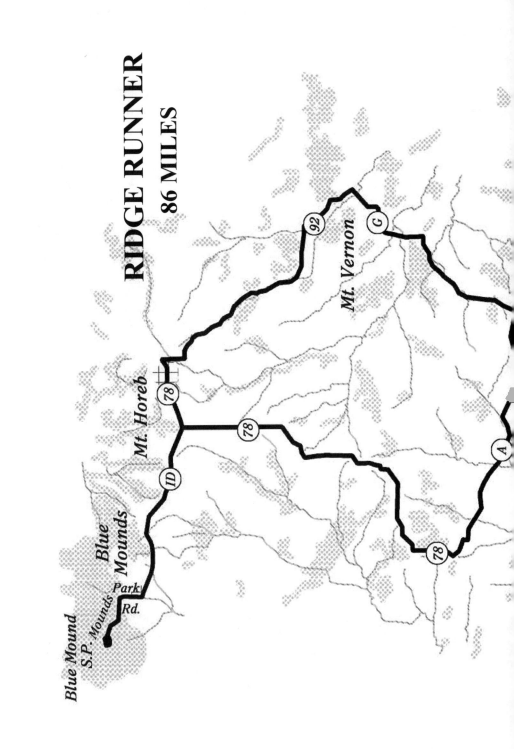

**RIDGE RUNNER**

**86 MILES**

Blue Mound
S.P. Mounds
Rd.
Park
Blue
Mounds
ID
Mt. Horeb
78
Mt. Vernon
92
G
78
A
78

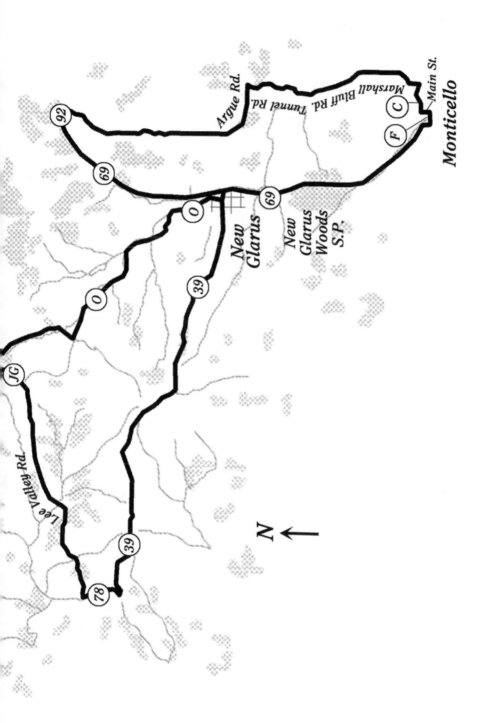

# RIDGE RUNNER - 86 MILES

Start in New Glarus.

| Road | Direction | | Miles |
|------|-----------|---|-------|
| Hwy 69 | Right | S | 4.9 |
| County F | Left | E | 0.2 |
| Main St. | Left | N | 0.2 |
| County C | Right | E | 1.5 |
| Marshall Bluff Rd. | Left | N | 2.7 |
| Tunnel Rd. | Left | N | 2.7 |
| Argue Rd. | Left | W | 5.0 |
| Hwy 92/69 | Left | W | 0.2 |
| Hwy 69 | Left | S | 4.3 |
| Hwy 39 | Right | W | 0.5 |
| County O | Right | N | 4.7 |
| Becomes County G | Straight | N | 8.5 |
| Hwy 92 | Left | W | 6.7 |
| Hwy 78 | Left | W | 1.6 |
| County ID | Straight | W | 4.0 |
| Mounds Park Rd. | Right | N | 1.0 |
| Follow to Blue Mound State Park | | | |
| Mounds Park Rd. | | S | 1.0 |
| County ID | Left | E | 4.0 |
| Hwy 78 | Right | S | 9.0 |
| County A | Left | E | 4.8 |
| County JG | Right | S | 2.1 |
| Lee Valley Rd. | Right | W | 5.2 |
| Hwy 78 | Left | S | 0.9 |
| Hwy 39 | Left | E | 10.3 |

# FOR MORE INFORMATION

**Blue Mound State Park** (state park sticker required)

608-437-5711

www.dnr.wi.gov/org/land/parks/specific/bluemound

**Monticello**

M & M Cafe 608-938-4890 www.monticellowi.com/M&MCafe/

Closed Sunday

**Mt. Horeb**

Chamber of Commerce 888-765-5929 www.trollway.com

Cave of the Mounds 608-437-3038 www.caveofthemounds.com

Year-round, call for hours

Little Norway 608-437-8211 www.littlenorway.com

May–October, fee

Mt. Horeb Area Historical Museum 608-437-6486

www.mounthoreb.org

Mustard Museum 608-437-3986 www.mustardmuseum.com

Daily 10a.m.–5p.m.

**New Glarus**

Chamber of Commerce  800-527-6838 www.swisstown.com

Green County Welcome Center 888-222-9111

www.greencounty.org

Chalet of the Golden Fleece 800-527-6838 May–October, fee

New Glarus Bakery 866-805-5536 www.newglarusbakery.com

New Glarus Brewing Company 608-527-5850

www.newglarusbrewing.com

Ruef's Meat Market 608-527-2554 www.ruefsmeatmarket.com

Swiss Historical Village 608-527-2317

www.swisshistoricalvillage.org

May–October, fee

---

Generally, I plan the routes and the guys lead. One eventful ride had the leader losing stuff out of his bags. Because I was in the back, it fell to me to retrieve the flying articles. By the time the leader got back to me, I was more than happy to hold up, for all to see, the underwear I'd recovered.

---

# 4  BADGER COUNTRY

Pendarvis

*Badger Country* takes you into the heart of the lead and zinc mining region where miners dug into the earth like badgers. Often the miners' first "homes" were depressions dug several feet into a hillside and covered with timbers for a roof. There was room enough to lie down and little else. As more miners arrived the cities of Argyle, Darlington, Mineral Point, and Blanchardville "grew up" around the needs of the mining industry. Today these towns have active historic committees and are renovating their downtowns as tourism becomes a bigger part of their economy.

## NOTES & HIGHLIGHTS

Start your day with a pastry from the New Glarus Bakery, which has been operating continuously since 1912, making it the state's oldest bakery. Then head out to Rustic Road 81, or Marty Road, which was laid out in the 1800s as a farm supply road. Five of the original farmhouses can still be seen.

County Roads A and G are wonderfully rolling roads at the top of wide open ridges with enough interest to prevent boredom, but not requiring too much effort to cruise. County F becomes a bit tighter on the way into Darlington.

The beautiful Lafayette County courthouse in Darlington was paid for by one person, Matt Murphy. At the turn of the century, he left his estate to build and pay all the costs of a new courthouse. Amazingly, there was $600 left when it was finished. A statue of Murphy stands in the rotunda.

Watch your mileage on County Road C, because the turnoff to Ferndale Road is on a curve and easily missed. Ferndale Road into Mineral Point is a tight, winding road with a good view of the native stone that has been quarried and used in local buildings.

At one time Mineral Point was the largest settlement in southwest Wisconsin, and much of it has been or is being restored. The entire city is on the National Register of Historic Places. The miners arriving from Cornwall, England, in the 1830s were excellent stone masons and built homes and cottages out of the native limestone and sandstone. Unfortunately, as the fortunes of mining declined, much of Mineral Point fell into disrepair. The cottages were scavenged to provide stone for foundations and other buildings. Much of the credit for beginning the restorations belongs to Robert Neal and Edgar Hellum. They brought several cottages to life on Shake Rag Street beginning in 1935. Their first house was named Pendarvis, after an estate in Cornwall. In 1970 the State Historical Society purchased Pendarvis and other buildings in the area, and the Pendarvis Historical Site was opened. Costumed guides present the history of the Cornish miners during Mineral Point's lead-mining heyday. Take the tour and find out how Shake Rag Street got its name.

Following on the heels of the historical renovations, Mineral Point began to attract artists in the 1940s and has become a haven for artisans. There are galleries and studios throughout the area, and many shops are located downtown.

From Mineral Point enjoy the sweeping curves of Highway 39 as it follows yet another wide open ridge top. Take the time to stop at Nick Englebert's Grandview located west of Hollandale. In the 1930s Englebert was a dairy farmer on a small scale, but when he broke his ankle he discovered a whole new avocation while recuperating. Nick began sculpting using items such as pieces of colored glass, mirrors, and colorful stones all held together with cement. His sculptures covered politics, fairy tales, his family, even the facade of his house. After his death in 1962, Grandview fell into disrepair but has since been restored and is free to visitors when the gate is open. The house is open in the summer. The parking lot is gravel but easily negotiated.

# BADGER COUNTRY
## 100 MILES

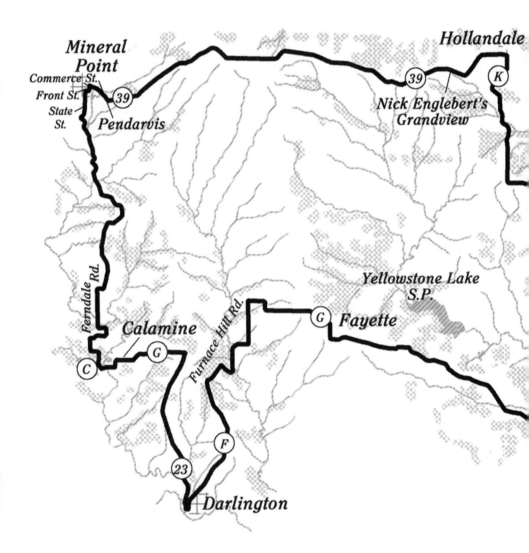

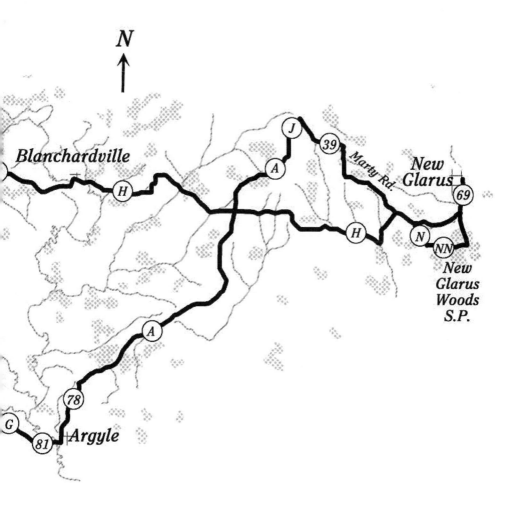

# BADGER COUNTRY - 100 MILES

Start in New Glarus.

| Road | Direction | | Miles |
|------|-----------|---|-------|
| Hwy 69 | | S | 1.9 |
| County NN | Right | W | 1.3 |
| County N | Right | N | 0.7 |
| County H | Left | W | 0.6 |
| Marty Rd. | Right | N | 2.9 |
| Hwy 39 | Left | W | 1.7 |
| County J | Left | S | 1.2 |
| County A | Right | S | 10.9 |
| Hwy 78 via Argyle | Left | S | 2.2 |
| Hwy 81 | Right | W | 0.4 |
| County G via Fayette | Right | W | 12.6 |
| Furnace Hill Rd. | Left | S | 4.7 |
| County F to Darlington | Right | S | 2.7 |
| Hwy 23 | Right | N | 4.9 |
| County G | Left | W | 4.0 |
| County C | Right | N | 1.1 |
| Ferndale Rd. | Right | N | 8.7 |
| State St. | Straight | N | 0.5 |
| Front St. | Right | E | 0.2 |
| Commerce St. | Left | N | 0.4 |
| Hwy 39 to Hollandale | Right | E | 13.6 |
| | Splits from Hwy 23 to the left | | |
| County K | Right | S | 5.2 |
| County F to Blanchardville | Left | E | 3.3 |
| Hwy 78 | Left | E | 0.2 |
| County H | Right | E | 13.7 |

# FOR MORE INFORMATION

**Argyle**
608-543-3113 www.argylewi.org
**Blanchardville**
608-523-2274 www.blanchardville.com
**Darlington**
Chamber of Commerce 608-776-3067
www.darlingtonwi.org/darlington_chamber.htm
**Mineral Point**
Chamber of Commerce 888-764-6894 www.mineralpoint.com
Pendarvis and Merry Christmas Mine  608-987-2122
www.wisconsinhistory.org/pendarvis
May–October, fee
**New Glarus**
Chamber of Commerce  800-527-6838 www.swisstown.com
Green County Welcome Center 888-222-9111
www.greencounty.org
Chalet of the Golden Fleece 800-527-6838
May–October, fee
New Glarus Bakery 866-805-5536 www.newglarusbakery.com
New Glarus Brewing Company 608-527-5850
www.newglarusbrewing.com
Ruef's Meat Market 608-527-2554 www.ruefsmeatmarket.com
Swiss Historical Village 608-527-2317
www.swisshistoricalvillage.org May–October, fee
**Yellowstone Lake State Park** (state park sticker required)
608-523-4427
www.dnr.wi.gov/org/land/parks/specific/yellowstone

---

Occasionally, my wanderings have put me on roads I've regretted. Wildlife Road in southwest Wisconsin was just such a road. It was barely visible from the county road, but paved–until I reached a point where I couldn't turn around. I found myself headed down a beautiful, treelined, curvy, hilly road of loose dirt, thinking if I ever see pavement again, I'll never do another bad thing in my life.

# 5 GALENA CIRCLE

I debated at length about beginning and ending this route in Galena, because it's in Illinois. In the end Galena won out because it's within the Driftless Area, and its mining history is closely tied to southwest Wisconsin. It's also a perfect destination spot, so the *Galena Circle* was born.

*Galena Circle* is my favorite route. The scenery is beautiful. The roads are challenging but not so challenging you think you've lost your riding skills. And there are historic points of interest in every community.

## NOTES & HIGHLIGHTS

Main St. - Galena

I would suggest you spend a weekend in Galena so you can explore this unique town. In the mid-1800s Galena's fortunes were dependent on lead mining and shipping. It was the major riverport in the area, and a thriving downtown was built along the Galena River. Mansions and homes were built up the steep bluffs on either side. As the ore declined so did the population of Galena—going from 14,000 people in the 1850s to 3,600 people today. The town languished until the 1960s, when an interest in historic restoration hit the community. Today, Galena survives on tourism. The painstakingly restored buildings house unique gift and antique shops along the curving Main Street. Make the effort (and I do mean effort) to walk the steps up the bluff on Green Street. You'll be rewarded with a great view of the surrounding area and a close look at the restored mansions.

If you ride into Galena from Highway 20, notice the gates at the entrance to Main Street. These flood gates are closed at least once every few years due to spring flooding. Don't despair if they happen to be closed when you

Galena flood

arrive: there will be signs directing you to alternate routes from the "high" side.

Okay, enough of all this walking and step climbing, it's time to head out on the Stagecoach Trail. At one time this was the main road bringing people, supplies, and most importantly the mail from Freeport, Illinois. It curves along the ridge, and the valleys are lush and green even in early spring when everything else seems to be brown. You'll turn on Elizabeth–Scales Mound Road and head into Scales Mound.

In the lead rush days, New Diggings was bigger than Chicago. Today its claim to fame is two general stores that are really taverns and the last remaining wooden church designed and built by Father Samuel Mazzuchelli in the mid-1800s. Although unassuming and unpainted, St. Augustine church is impressive in its simplicity. You may notice that the siding has been done so that it would look like stone if the church were painted.

Father Mazzuchelli was an Italian missionary of the

St. Augustine Church

Dominican Order of Preachers. He founded churches and schools in 20 area settlements, as well as the Dominican Sisters in Sinsinawa before his death in 1864. He is currently being considered for sainthood.

County Road O weaves its way into Shullsburg, which was founded in 1827 and named after Jesse Shull. Legend has it that while eating lunch beside a stream, the fur trader spotted a badger digging into the earth. When he went to investigate, Shull saw the badger had uncovered lead ore. Whether you believe that tale or not, the area around Shullsburg accounted for 85 percent of the nation's lead output in its peak years. While lead put Shullsburg on the map, the boom created by the railroad's coming in 1881 is responsible for its growth and downtown buildings. Father Mazzuchelli influenced the naming of many of the town's streets, including Charity, Judgment, Hope, and Virtue.

Shullsburg is home to the natural phenomenon called "Gravity Hill." Located on County U two miles south of town, this optical illusion makes the road appear to go uphill while your stopped motorcycle will roll backward downhill.

North of Shullsburg, County O stops winding and starts rolling. There are some major roller coaster hills with great views of silos standing sentry over the many farms dotting the landscape.

First capitol - Belmont

At the intersection of County Roads G and B is the Wisconsin Territory's first capitol. In 1836 legislators met for 46 days and passed 42 laws to put together the new territorial government. The representatives accomplished much in a short period of time because they were not happy about the primitive conditions they encountered in the early Belmont. The territorial capitol was moved to Mineral Point, where it remained for two years before moving to Madison permanently.

Platte Mound is on County B. When you get beyond it, pull over and look back. The world's largest "M," made of whitewashed stone, is on the side of the mound. The "M" was originally constructed in 1937 by students of the Wisconsin Mining Trade School. Its upkeep is an annual project for engineering students at the UW-Platteville.

Platteville has been home to an institution of higher learning since 1839. The Platteville Academy became the first teacher's college in the state in 1927 and merged in 1959 with the School of Mines to eventually become the UW-Platteville. In addition to a proud academic history, the university previously hosted the Chicago Bears summer training camp.

Highway 81 into Cassville is a nice change of pace. The curves are fast and wide along the ridge tops and through the valleys. In Beetown the road slides into a cool, narrow valley with imposing rock bluffs on each side.

Nearly midway Highway 81 passes through Lancaster, "Home of the Dome." The Grant County courthouse has a strikingly beautiful octagonal copper and glass dome.

Grant County courthouse

And you don't have to leave the route to see it.

The small Mississippi River town of Cassville has a surprising number of attractions. Nelson Dewey State Park was named after the territory's first governor. In 1860 he returned to Cassville and created an estate named Stonefield. His mansion was reconstructed after a fire, but some of the estate's original stone fence can be seen in the park. The overlook in the park has spectacular views of the river and of Stonefield Village. This State Historical Site contains replica buildings depicting village life in the 1890s.

If you'd like to get closer to the river, there is a ferry that will take you to the Iowa side. It's always a good idea to call ahead for its operating hours. You can stay on the ferry and return to Cassville or continue into Iowa. (Note: the first mile of road in Iowa is a dirt, rutted, single lane.)

Highway 133 leaves Cassville and the river behind as it climbs and curls along the bluff carved by the river (which is just beyond view). The pace is fast as the road swoops into Potosi. This town boasts the world's longest main street without an intersection as the valley walls rise sharply behind the houses. It's also home to St. John's Mine, where Harry, the owner, gives the most delightful, informative tour. The National Brewery Museum is expected to open in 2008 in the restored Potosi Brewery building.

The Grotto - Dickeyville

A must stop is the Grotto at the Holy Ghost Parish in Dickeyville. From 1925 to 1930 the parish priest, Father Matthias Wernerus, enlisted the help of volunteers to sculpt several shrines and monuments. His materials were cement, stone and brightly colored objects. From all over the world people sent him seashells, marbles, pottery, and, among other items, a large assortment of stick shift knobs. All of these objects were used in Father Wernerus's designs to create beautiful mosaics.

On County Z before you cross Highway 11 sits Sinsinawa Mound, home to the Sinsinawa Dominican Sisters. Their very popular kitchen is known for caramel rolls, cinnamon bread, and several other varieties of bread. Purchase a special treat to eat here or on the road.

Sinsinawa Road is a narrow, twisting farm road through a shallow valley. At one place, a short section of road appears to dead-end into a farmyard; this is only because the road is usually a mess of soil or manure. Unless you like cleaning manure from your bike and clothing, do not take this road on a wet spring day.

At the Wisconsin-Illinois border on Highway 80 there is a historical marker. This spot is the "Point of the Beginning." Since 1831 every public land survey in Wisconsin begins at this point. Part of the original survey marker can be seen at the Cunningham Museum in Lancaster.

Sinsinawa Road

The wonderful thing about traveling is the people you get to meet along the way. The motorcycle is a great conversation starter. And if you're not in too much of a hurry, people are more than willing to tell you their story. Everyone has one.

I recently began taking photos of these storytellers. At first I felt a little awkward about asking, but most people don't seem to mind. Actually, unless they're in the Witness Protection Program, people seem puzzled that anyone would find them interesting.

Pictures of where I've been are nice, but it's the people who ultimately make the journey a special one. I love looking back at the photos and remembering why these faces are so special.

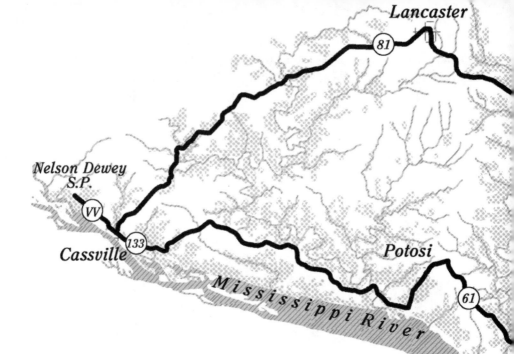

# GALENA CIRCLE
## 149 MILES

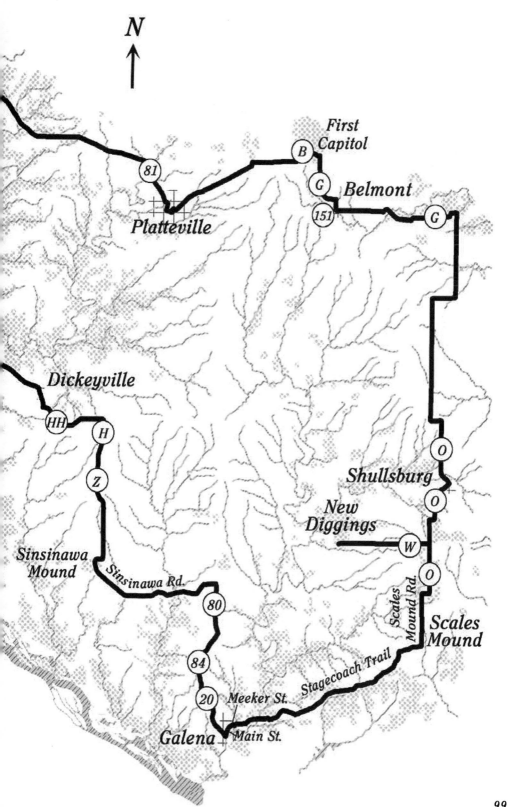

N

First
Capitol

B

G

Belmont

81

151

G

Platteville

Dickeyville

HH

H

O

Z

Shullsburg

New
Diggings

O

Sinsinawa
Mound

Sinsinawa Rd.

W

80

O

Scales
Mound Rd.

Scales
Mound

84

20

Meeker St.

Stagecoach Trail

Galena

Main St.

# GALENA CIRCLE - 149 MILES

Start in Galena, Illinois.

| Road | Direction | | Miles |
|------|-----------|---|-------|
| Main St. | | N | 0.7 |
| Meeker St. | Right | E | 0.3 |
| Stagecoach Trail | Straight | E | 9.9 |
| Elizabeth–Scales Mound Rd. | Left | N | 2.9 |
| Becomes Franklin St. while in Scales Mound. Turn right on South St., left across RR crossing, left again to Franklin St. | | | |
| County O | Straight | N | 2.0 |
| County W | Left | W | 4.6 |
| St. Augustine Church, New Diggings. Follow the signs | | | |
| County W | Right | E | 4.6 |
| County O via Shullsburg | Left | N | 3.0 |
| County O/Hwy 11 | Right | E | 0.2 |
| County O | Left | N | 12.4 |
| County G | Left | W | 5.6 |
| Hwy 151 | Right | N | 0.6 |
| County G | Left | W | 3.1 |
| County B | Left | W | 6.0 |
| Broadway St. in Platteville | Straight | W | 0.7 |
| Main St. | Right | N | 0.1 |
| Water St. | Left | W | 0.1 |
| Hwy 81 in Lancaster | Right | N | 16.0 |
| Hwy 81 in Cassville | Straight | W | 18.9 |
| Hwy 133 | Right | N | 0.6 |
| County VV | Left | N | 3.0 |
| Lookout from Nelson Dewey S.P. | | | |
| County VV | Left | S | 3.0 |
| Hwy 133 via Potosi | | W | 19.6 |
| Hwy 61 via Dickeyville | Right | S | 7.7 |

| Road | Direction | | Miles |
|---|---|---|---|
| County HH | Left | E | 3.2 |
| County H | Right | S | 2.6 |
| County Z, Cross Hwy 11 | Left | S | 3.8 |
| Sinsinawa Rd. | Left | E | 6.1 |

Follows the Ill./Wis. border, and to add confusion is called W. Doyle Rd. in Ill.

| | | | |
|---|---|---|---|
| Hwy 80 Becomes Hwy 84 | Right | S | 4.6 |

Point of Beginning Historical Marker on left just before state line

| | | | |
|---|---|---|---|
| Hwy 20 | Straight | S | 3.4 |
| Main St. | Left | N | |

Sinsinawa Mound

# FOR MORE INFORMATION

**Belmont First Capitol Historic Site**
608-987-2122 www.wisconsinhistory.org/firstcapitol
June–Labor Day

**Cassville**
Cassville Tourism 608-725-5855 www.cassville.org
Car ferry 608-725-5180
May–October. Call for hours, fee
Nelson Dewey State Park (state park sticker required)
608-725-5374
www.dnr.wi.gov/org/land/parks/specific/nelsondewey
Stonefield Village 608-725-5210
www.wisconsinhistory.org/stonefield
May–October, fee

**Dickeyville**
www.grantcounty.org/ci/dickeyville
The Grotto 608-568-3119 May–September

**Galena**
Galena/Jo Daviess County Convention & Visitors Bureau
877-464-2536 www.galena.org
Comprehensive online visitor's guide

**Grant County**
866-472-6894 www.grantcounty.org/visitor

**Lancaster**
Chamber of Commerce 608-723-2820
www.lancasterwisconsin.com
Cunningham Museum 608-723-2287
Monday–Saturday afternoons
Grant County Courthouse
Open during business hours Monday–Friday

**Platteville**
Chamber of Commerce 608-348-8888
www.platteville.com
Mitchell-Rountree Stone Cottage
Memorial Day–Labor Day

Rollo Jamison Museum & Mining Museum 608-348-3301
www.mining.jamison.museum
May–October Guided tours
November–April, self-guided tours
UW-Platteville
www.uwplatt.edu

**Potosi**

Chamber of Commerce 608-763-2261
www.potosiwisconsin.com
National Brewery/Potosi Brewery Museums
www.potosibrewery.com
St. John Mine 608-763-2121
May–October

**Shullsburg**

www.shullsburgwisconsin.org
Includes directions to Gravity Hill
Badger Mine & Museum 608-965-4860
Memorial Day–Labor Day

**Sinsinawa Mound Center**

Dominican Sisters 608-748-4411 www.sinsinawa.org

---

I seem to learn something everytime I drop my bike. One of those times was in Galena. I realized as I started up a hill that I was going the wrong way, so I attempted to turn around. Now, I probably could have made it under power, but instead I stopped and attempted to walk the bike around. My downhill leg wasn't long enough to balance the bike and down I went. Out of nowhere about twelve kids appeared to watch my friends and me pick up the offending machine.

# IV - COULEE COUNTRY

A TALE OF THREE RIVERS - 182 MILES
OCOOCH MOUNTAINS - 83 MILES
ACROSS THE BORDER - 142 MILES
MINDORO CUT - 73 MILES

# IV - COULEE COUNTRY

The Coulee region shares the same unglaciated geologic features—long winding ridges, steep valleys, and many twisting streams and rivers—as the Driftless Area, but it seldom goes by that name. Instead the section north of the Wisconsin River became known as Coulee Country,

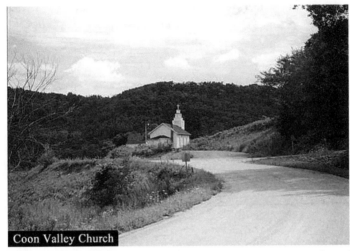

Coon Valley Church

or God's Country. "Coulee" refers to the short, steep valleys named by French fur trappers in the late 1700s.

The natural resources were much different than further south, and a different group of settlers immigrated to this area. Many nationalities were reflected in the regional names: Mormon Coulee, Irish Ridge, German Coulee, Bohemian Ridge, and Norwegian Coulee. Germans and Norwegians accounted for the largest immigrant groups.

From 1850 to 1890 there was a huge demand for lumber to build the homes and towns in the country's westward expansion. The vast tracts of timber brought Germans and Bohemians as well as others to the Coulee region. While the sound of axes could be heard clearing the pine forests of northern Wisconsin, Coulee Country was spared to some degree because its forests were mostly hardwood—oak and hickory. (Soft pine was the preferred wood because it was easier to use and resistant to water rot.) The timber operations in this area were focused on milling and on the services necessary to bring the northern pine down the Mississippi and Wisconsin Rivers. Not only was water in abundance to run sawmills, it was also available for the German breweries in the La Crosse area.

Farming was by far the largest portion of the economy. Norwegians arrived in the 1830s to establish farms on terrain that reminded them of their homeland. Most planted wheat, until those yields began to drop in the late 1800s, and then they switched to dairying. The first dairy product was butter made for home consumption. The excess was sold at market but was of such poor quality it was used for wagon wheel grease. With advances in technology, the quality improved and Wisconsin butter and cheese began to compete with the New England states. The phrase "Wisconsin—America's Dairyland" was coined in the 1930s, and the Coulee region became one of the major producers of cheese in Wisconsin. (From 1895 to 1967, colored margarine was banned in the state to increase butter sales.)

Just as in the 1800s water is still a major resource in the Coulee Country, but now it is used for recreational purposes. The many crooked rivers provide wonderful canoeing possibilities, and the plentiful streams provide excellent trout fishing. In fact, there are over 200 miles of trout streams.

**Coulee Country** has excellent roads for motorcycling in part because of the diversity. From the wide, swooping curves along the Mississippi River to the narrow twisting valleys that follow the Kickapoo River, the scene changes constantly.

There are four routes totaling 480 miles in **Coulee Country**:

- *A Tale of Three Rivers*
- *Ocooch Mountains*
- *Across the Border*
- *Mindoro Cut*

All the routes start in Cashton, located in the middle of the largest Amish community in Wisconsin. Cashton began as a stage stop on a route to the Mississippi River. Later, it was a stop on a spur of the Milwaukee Railroad built by William Henry Harrison Cash.

You can make the Ages Past Country Inn and Restaurant an overnight stop. This former Catholic rectory has been wonderfully refurbished by Carl and Barbara Bargabos into a beautiful Victorian bed and breakfast. The Cashton Mercantile provides a look into the Amish community with tours and handcrafted gifts made by the local Amish and other artisans. Down a Country Road features a cluster of little shops on the Kuderer farm. Built by surrounding Amish craftsman, the shops feature items such as furniture, quilts, jams, honey, rugs, and baskets.

# 1  A TALE OF THREE RIVERS

*A Tale of Three Rivers* is about the Mississippi, Wisconsin, and Kickapoo Rivers. The Great River Road (marked by green pilotwheel signs) follows the Mississippi River from its headwaters in Minnesota to the Gulf of Mexico. It is one of the oldest and longest scenic byways in the country. The scenery on this route was created 14,000 years ago by glacial runoff through the uplands of the Coulee region. The five-hundred-foot bluffs on both sides of the river are the direct result.

The Wisconsin River was also created by glacial runoff after an ice dam broke, unleashing waters from an ancient lake. Sand, gravel, and silt from the rushing waters covered some areas of the riverbed 150 feet high, and as the flooding decreased the river cut multiple terraces through it. The confluence of the Mississippi and the Wisconsin Rivers is just south of Prairie du Chien.

The Kickapoo River meanders its way south through the coulees to join the Wisconsin River at Wauzeka. This is one of the most crooked rivers in the world. There are 100 river miles of twists and turns in 33 linear miles.

## NOTES & HIGHLIGHTS

Amish

There are no coulees named for Amish settlers, but a sizeable community has grown in the Cashton area since 1966. On Saturday mornings, you can sit in town and watch the horses and buggies clip-clop past on the way to marketing. Traveling County Roads D and P is like traveling back in time. The Amish do things the "old-fashioned way," without the aid of power equipment. Here you'll see wash on the line, children mowing the lawn with reel mowers, and farmers planting and harvesting with teams of horses. Signs at the ends of driveways advertise quilts, furniture, jams, and baked goods. There are no Sunday sales, as the Amish congregate at neighboring farms for church services, fellowship, and dinner. I had to laugh one day when I found myself gawking at a buggy full of kids. I realized they were gawking back at me and my motorcycle.

As you round a curve on County P, a ski jump suddenly appears. A few more curves brings you to the Snowflake Ski and Golf Club. And, there really is a ski jump, a very tall, 114 meter ski jump that has been in use since 1923. In the summer the runway becomes a nine-hole golf course.

A short detour off County P onto County PI will take you to Norskedalen (Norwegian Valley) Nature and Heritage Center. This 400-acre preserve features reconstructed log buildings representing area farms. The Norwegian settlers' life is carefully preserved here. The road into the center and the parking lot are paved.

Coon Valley, as you might guess, was named for the many raccoons in the area. This is a lovely little town with several gift shops to explore. For dinner, DiSciascio's offers fabulous Italian meals.

Highway 162 is a favorite of mine, as it curves and twists with the contours of the land. It follows Coon Creek from Coon Valley into Stoddard where it joins with the Great River Road, or Highway 33. Many of the Norwegian settlers arrived in Stoddard and walked along the creek, selecting farm sites as they went.

Stoddard River Park provides a good view of the river at one of its widest points, nearly four miles. Lock and Dam #8 in Genoa flooded what had been farmland and woodlot. View the river from another perspective by taking the winding road

Dairyland Power Plant

up a 500-foot bluff to Old Settler's Overlook.

From Stoddard to Prairie du Chien, it is 47 miles of Great River Road. It is a road with wide, sweeping, fast curves and views that make it hard to keep your eyes on the road. One of my most memorable moments came when an eagle flew above me as if to guide me on my journey. Fortunately, there are pull offs at regular intervals.

Cigar store Indian - Lynxville

There are two locks and dams: #8 at Genoa and #9 at Lynxville. They were built in the late 1930s by the Army Corps of Engineers to provide inexpensive, efficient transportation by barge. Today they continue to allow 90 million tons of cargo to pass between St. Louis and St. Paul. Both provide viewing platforms to observe the locks in action.

South of Genoa the Dairyland Power Plant looms over the river. It was one of the first nuclear powered electric generators in the nation, running from 1969 to 1987. For economic reasons the generator is now coal-fired.

Up and down the river there are Black Hawk parks, restaurants, hotels, and monuments. Black Hawk was a Sauk Indian chief who fought the white government and settlers over treaties that granted the land east of the Mississippi to the United States. The Black Hawk Wars ended in 1832 near the town of Victory, when Black Hawk's starving followers attempted to escape across the river to Minnesota. The battle is known as the Bad Axe Massacre, because many women, children, and elders were shot or drowned in their attempts to flee. There is a historical marker just north of DeSoto commemorating this battle.

Continuing south, the River Road seems to hang from the bluff, with the railroad tracks and the river below. You will pass through the city of Ferryville, which began life as Humblebush but was later renamed because it was the base of the ferry between Humblebush and Lansing, Iowa. Further south is Lynxville, where you'll find the largest cigar store

Indian at the Black Hawk Bait and Tackle.

Your trip along the Mississippi ends in Prairie du Chien (prairie of the dogs) which is the second oldest European settlement in Wisconsin. (Green Bay is the oldest.) Villa Louis is a short distance off the route and is an excellent stop. This State Historical Site is the former Victorian country estate of Hercules Dousman, Wisconsin's first millionaire. Sitting atop a mound, it has a commanding view of the Mississippi River.

Wauzeka is where the Kickapoo River meets the Wisconsin River and where you will turn north onto one of the nicest roads. Highway 131 has it all: tight curves through the rock bluffs of the Kickapoo Valley, tree canopies, picture postcard views atop long ridges, and little traffic. There aren't many historical points or reasons to stop. This is just the kind of road meant for a motorcycle.

You will want to stop in Gays Mills, especially the last full weekend of September for Apple Festival. The bluffs of this Kickapoo Valley town are perfect for growing apples. Since 1911 there have been over 1,000 acres of orchards planted.

Gays Mills

After the nice ride on Highways 171 and 27 with their broad curves and never ending vistas, I must admit Highway 82 west of Fargo is a little bit boring. Fortunately you will be rewarded with your turn onto County N. On a hot day this is the best place to be as it descends into a cool, steep valley and winds between the rock walls. It's beautiful in the late afternoon with the sun playing peekaboo through the trees.

The first thing you notice when you arrive in Westby is the Tourist Information Center. It is located in the Stabbur (Norwegian for a farm storehouse). This particular one was moved from the nearby Monroe Johnson farm. The Stabbur is open early spring to late fall.

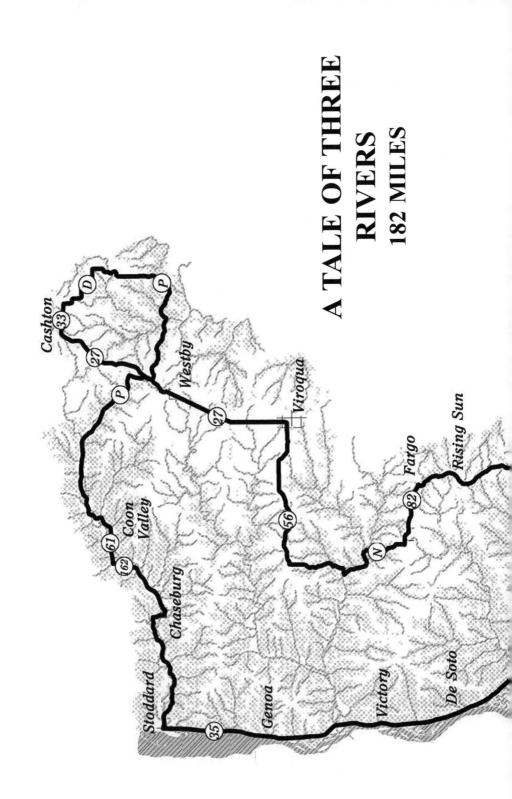

A TALE OF THREE
RIVERS
182 MILES

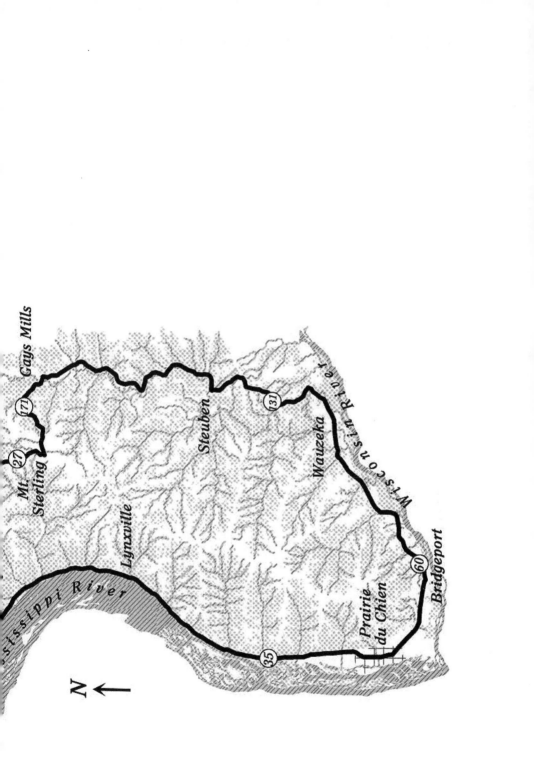

Gays Mills

77

27

Mt. Sterling

Lynxville

Steuben

131

Wauzeka

*Wisconsin River*

Bridgeport

60

Prairie du Chien

35

*Mississippi River*

N ←

# A TALE OF THREE RIVERS - 182 MILES

Start in Cashton.

| Road | Direction | | Miles |
|---|---|---|---|
| Hwy 33 | | E | 0.9 |
| County D | Right | S | 7.0 |
| County P | Right | W | 6.2 |
| Hwy 27 | Right | N | 0.5 |
| County P | Left | W | 12.0 |
| Hwy 61 via Coon Valley | Right | W | 1.4 |
| Hwy 162 via Chaseburg | Left | S | 12.0 |
| Hwy 35 to Genoa | Left | S | 7.2 |
| Hwy 35 to Victory | Straight | S | 6.6 |
| Hwy 35 to DeSoto | Straight | S | 4.6 |
| Hwy 35 to Ferryville | Straight | S | 7.3 |
| Hwy 35 to Lynxville | Straight | S | 8.3 |
| Hwy 35 to Prairie du Chien | Straight | S | 15.0 |
| Hwy 35 to Bridgeport | Straight | E | 5.7 |
| Hwy 60 via Wauzeka | Left | E | 12.1 |
| Hwy 131 to Steuben | Left | N | 7.1 |
| Hwy 131 to Gays Mills | Right | N | 12.0 |
| Hwy 171 to Mt. Sterling | Left | W | 5.5 |
| Hwy 27 to Fargo | Right | N | 16.1 |
| Hwy 82 | Left | W | 3.5 |
| County N | Right | N | 8.3 |
| Hwy 56 to Viroqua | Right | E | 8.5 |
| Hwy 27/14/61 to Westby | Left | N | 7.5 |
| Hwy 27 | Straight | N | 7.0 |
| Hwy 33 | Right | E | 0.1 |

# FOR MORE INFORMATION

**Cashton**
>www.bikesandberries.com/cashton.html
>Ages Past Country Inn & Restaurant  608-654-5950
>www.agespast.net
>Cashton Mercantile 608-654-5387 www.cashtonmercantile.com
>Down a Country Road 608-654-5318
>www.downacountryroad.com

**Coon Valley**
>DiSciascio's Coon Creek Inn  888-452-3182 or 608-452-3182
>>Closed Monday year round, and Tuesday October–May
>Norskedalen Nature & Heritage Center 608-452-3424
>www.norskedalen.org

**Gays Mills**
>www.gaysmills.org

**Great River Road**
>www.wigreatriverroad.org
>www.greatriver.com

**Kickapoo Valley**
>www.kickapoovalley.org

**Prairie du Chien**
>Chamber of Commerce 800-732-1673
>www.prairieduchien.org
>Cabela's 608-326-5600  www.cabelas.com
>Ft. Crawford Museum 608-326-6960
>www.fortcrawfordmuseum.com
>May–October, fee
>Villa Louis 608-326-2721 www.wisconsinhistory.org/villalouis
>May–October, fee

**Viroqua**
>Chamber of Commerce 608-637-2575
>www.viroqua-wisconsin.com

**Wauzeka**
>Kickapoo Indian Caverns 608-875-7723
>www.kickapooindiancaverns.com

**Westby**
>Tourist Information Center–Stabbur 608-634-4011
>www.westbywi.com

# 2 OCOOCH MOUNTAINS

What? You didn't know there are mountains in Wisconsin? It will take a stretch of the imagination for some people, but the Ocooch

Coulee Valley farm

Mountains are some pretty big hills for this state. Ocooch refers to the ridges found by French explorers in the northern Kickapoo Valley. After you navigate this route you can brag you did some mountain riding.

Some of the mountain roads I've ridden haven't been as challenging or as beautiful. The route seems to rise and twist and weave through every valley in the region. The hollows are draped with trees, and the rocky outcrops have been eroded into many shapes. You'll have the roads mostly to yourself, except in the fall when traffic increases for "leaf peeping."

## NOTES & HIGHLIGHTS

*Ocooch Mountains* begins in Cashton and follows Highway 33 east to Ontario. This is one of the recommended roads for seeing the Amish way of life.

Ontario is becoming quite the canoeing center. The Kickapoo River is great for canoeists who want a good paddle but not a challenge. There are at least four places to rent canoes, and they all provide shuttle service. A popular trip is from Ontario to Wildcat Mountain State Park, which takes about three hours. You could do some canoeing and still finish this route.

The Wildcat Mountain State Park observation point has a fantastic view of the Kickapoo Valley. Two notes of caution: Wildcat Mountain allows horses, so be careful the iron pony doesn't meet the live one. And the exit from the park is a bit difficult. The road is canted steeply down, which makes the turn onto the main road difficult. I usually go wide left into the RV lane.

From the State Park to Hillsboro, the highway follows Cheyenne Valley. Beginning in 1855 this was home to one of the first African American settlements in Wisconsin. By all reports, the valley was one of harmony between the races and ethnic groups. As the isolation of the area decreased by the 1930s, however, the separate ethnic communities began to deteriorate also. Today there isn't much left but a historical marker on the southeast side of Hillsboro.

Among the many ethnic groups that settled in Hillsboro, the Czechs made the most lasting impression. The heritage celebration called Cesky Den is held the second weekend in June.

Yuba is so isolated I'm amazed people find their way in and out. It was one of the few places in the area where I felt like a stranger. Beaver Creek Drive and County Road C leading to Yuba are narrow and full of tight turns.

You may be tempted to blow by Pier Park in Rockbridge, but don't because you'll miss one of Wisconsin's biggest natural bridges. Stop to walk through the rock fissure to the Pine River, where the water has undercut the sandstone leaving a beautiful overhang. This is a tranquil, magical place, and on a hot summer day it is one of the coolest places around.

County Road D is a fantastic road to ride, as it weaves its way back through the Ocooch Mountains to Amish country. If you ride this route in August, you will have the opportunity to see horsedrawn threshing equipment being used and haystacks being formed by hand. Also, like kids everywhere, the Amish children can't resist showing an interest in the passing motorcycles.

On the way to school

# OCOOCH MOUNTAINS
## 83 MILES

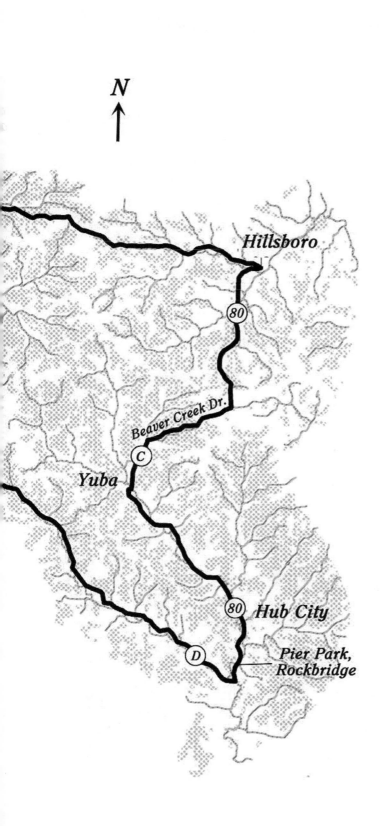

# OCOOCH MOUNTAINS - 83 MILES

Start in Cashton.

| Road | Direction | | Miles |
|---|---|---|---|
| Hwy 33 to Ontario | | E | 10.2 |
| Hwy 33 to Wildcat Mtn. | Straight | E | 2.7 |
| Hwy 33 to Hillsboro | Left | E | 13.7 |
| Hwy 80 | Right | S | 2.8 |
| Beaver Creek Dr. (3rd right from County Q) becomes | | | |
| County C via Yuba | Right | W | 13.7 |
| Hwy 80 to Pier Park, Rockbridge | Right | S | 3.2 |
| County D | Right | W | 17.4 |
| Hwy 82 via LaFarge | Left | W | 4.8 |
| County D | Right | W | 13.6 |
| Hwy 33 to Cashton | Left | W | 1.0 |

Pier Park - Rockbridge

# FOR MORE INFORMATION

**Cashton**
www.bikesandberries.com/cashton.html
Ages Past Country Inn & Restaurant  608-654-5950
www.agespast.net
Cashton Mercantile 608-654-5387 www.cashtonmercantile.com
Down a Country Road 608-654-5318
www.downacountryroad.com

**Hillsboro**
City Clerk 608-489-2521
www.hillsborowi.com

**Kickapoo Valley**
www.kickapoovalley.org

**Ontario**
Village Clerk 608-337-4381
Drifty's Canoe Rental 608-337-4288
Kickapoo Paddle Inn 608-337-4726
Mr. Duck Canoe Rental 608-337-4711
Titanic Canoe Rental 608-337-4551

**Vernon County**
www.wisconline.com/counties/vernon

**Wildcat Mountain State Park** (state park sticker required)
608-337-4775 www.dnr.wi.gov/org/land/parks/specific/wildcat

---

Women often fear they have to be perfect on the bike or they will be judged more harshly because they're women. I've found this is mostly in our heads and not reality, but I've also found preparedness helps take some of the anxiety out of the ride. Routes with good directions and maps go a long way toward that end.

I also accept help when I need it. I may not need a man to ride my motorcycle, but I might need his help to pick it up.

Great River Road sign

The Ojibwe recognized the importance of the Mississippi River by calling it Missi Sipi or "Great River." The Great River Road travels both sides of the river from its tributaries in Canada to its end in the Gulf of Mexico—over 3,000 miles. The road was legislated in 1938 with the purpose of preserving the historical, natural, and recreational resources along its path. *Across the Border* lets you discover these unique features in three states: Iowa, Minnesota, and Wisconsin.

## NOTES & HIGHLIGHTS

Heading south from Cashton, you'll arrive in Westby. This small town, which sits on a ridge between the Mississippi and Kickapoo River Valleys, was settled in 1843 by Norwegian immigrants. From the Velkommen sign at the edge of town to the architecture, the Norwegian influence is still felt. Syttende Mai (May 17) is held each year on the weekend closest to May 17 to celebrate Norway's Constitution Day.

From Westby along Highways 14 and 162, the ridges and coulees are dotted with small farms first claimed by the Norwegian settlers who walked east from Stoddard. While cows are plentiful, every now and then you will notice what seems like an odd crop for Wisconsin: tobacco. This cash crop has been planted since the 1870s.

Follow the Great River Road signs on Highway 35 to just south of DeSoto. (See *Tale of Three Rivers* for highlights.) Highway 82 crosses the river on the Black Hawk Bridge, the only bridge between La Crosse and Prairie du Chien. This is an old, steep, narrow, rather short, steel-deck bridge that dumps you into Lansing, Iowa, at the foot of Mt. Hosmer.

A little detour to the left takes you into Lansing. Follow the signs to Mt. Hosmer, where you can reach the summit via a steep, winding road. The first turn into the park is a sharp steep right.

Just south of New Albin is Fish Farm Mounds State Preserve. This is one of the few remaining sites preserving the ancient Woodland Indian burial mounds. There are 28 in this small primitive park.

Highway 26 is part of the Great River Road system, but the Mississippi has receded from view. From Lansing nearly to La Crescent, the river is filled with sloughs, small backwater channels, wooded islands, and marshes. Just like the river, this is a lazy, unhurried road.

The Mississippi comes back into full view in La Crescent, which is best known for its apple orchards and the Hiawatha Apple Blossom Scenic Route. County Roads 29 and 12 from La Crescent to Dakota make up one of the most scenic routes in Minnesota. The road winds up through the neatly planted rows of apple orchards and runs along the top of a 600-foot bluff. The views are spectacular.

Interstate 94 runs between Dakota and north of La Crescent along the Mississippi. You'll want to continue along the river on Highway 14, where you pass over the water into La Crosse.

La Crosse's first settler was Nathan Myrick, a young man of eighteen who built a trading post on the Mississippi River in 1842. It was a quiet town until the 1850s, when lumbering brought on a boom. Logs floated down from the north on the Mississippi, Black, and La Crosse Rivers, which all converge here. There was a steady buzz of saws. La Crosse was also home to several breweries, with G. Heileman being the largest until its closure in the early 1990s. An independent brewery currently occupies the Heileman facility and offers tours.

Just off the route is Grandad Bluff, a popular spot from which to view the river.

Highway 33 returning to Cashton is scenic and very winding as it runs along the ridge.

Fishing near the Black Hawk Bridge

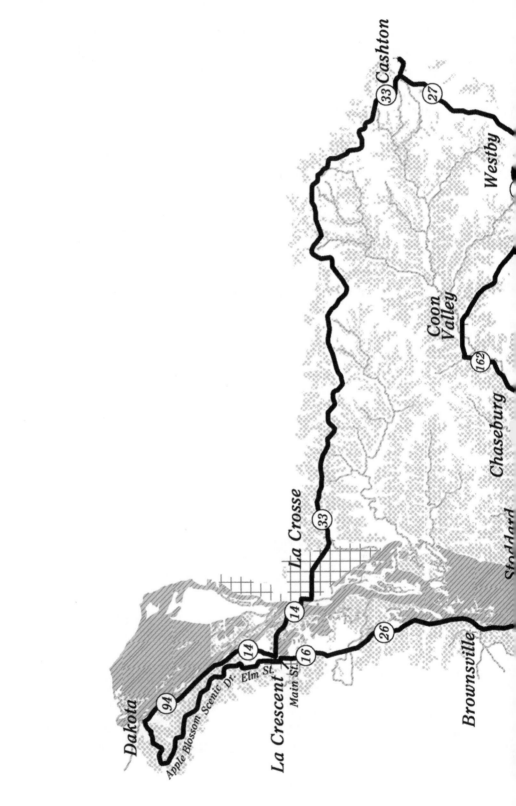

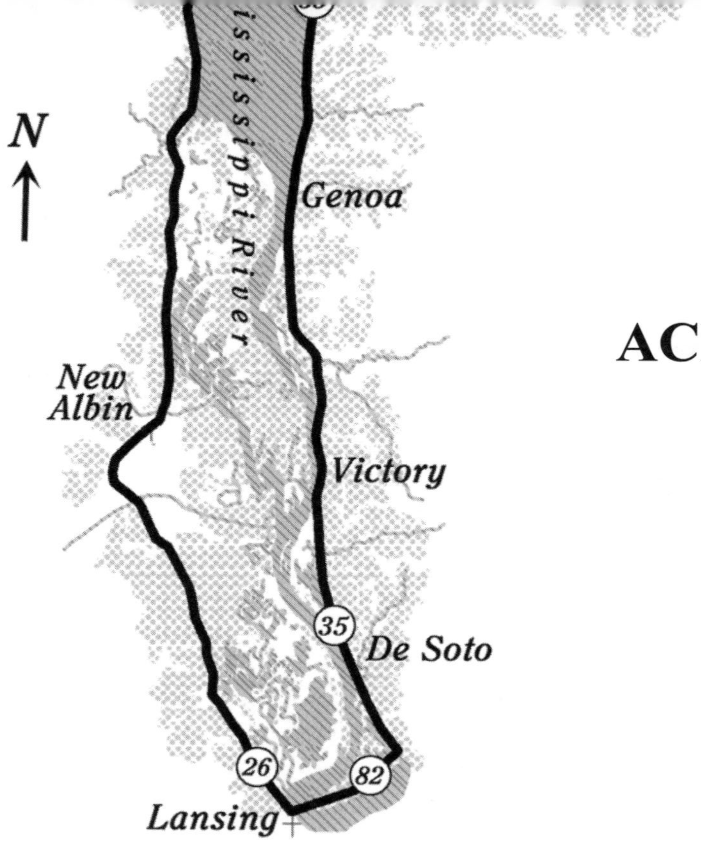

# ACROSS THE BORDER
## 142 MILES

Genoa

Mississippi River

Victory

De Soto

New Albin

35

82

26

Lansing

N

# ACROSS THE BORDER - 142 MILES

Start in Cashton.

| Road | Direction | | Miles |
|------|-----------|---|-------|
| Hwy 33 | | W | 0.8 |
| Hwy 27 to Westby | Left | S | 6.9 |
| Hwy 14 via Coon Valley | Right | W | 10.7 |
| Hwy 162 to Stoddard | Left | S | 12.6 |
| Hwy 35 to Genoa | Left | S | 7.2 |
| Hwy 35 to Victory | Straight | S | 6.6 |
| Hwy 35 to De Soto | Straight | S | 4.6 |
| Hwy 35 | Straight | S | 2.2 |
| Hwy 82 to Lansing, Iowa | Right | W | 2.8 |
| Hwy 26 to New Albin | Right | N | 13.0 |
| Hwy 26 to Brownsville, Minn. | Straight | N | 12.3 |
| Hwy 26 | Straight | N | 7.2 |
| Hwy 16 to La Crescent | Right | N | 2.5 |
| Apple Blossom Scenic Dr. | (Stoplight at Jct. 14/16) | | |
| S. Walnut St./CR6 | Left | W | 0.2 |
| Main St. | Left | W | 0.6 |
| Elm St./CR 29 | Right | N | 8.3 |
| CR 12 to Dakota | Right | E | 2.3 |
| I-94 | Right | S | 4.6 |
| Hwy 14 to La Crescent | Exit 275 | S | 2.7 |
| Hwy 14 to La Crosse | Left | E | 4.7 |
| Hwy 33 (Turn after brewery) | Left | E | 29.2 |

There's nothing more heartwarming than riding past a little boy or girl who then turns toward the motorcycle to wave with mouth open in awe and eyes glistening with excitement.

# FOR MORE INFORMATION

**Cashton**

www.bikesandberries.com/cashton.html
Ages Past Country Inn & Restaurant  608-654-5950
www.agespast.net
Cashton Mercantile 608-654-5387 www.cashtonmercantile.com
Down a Country Road 608-654-5318
www.downacountryroad.com

**Coon Valley**

DiSciascio's Coon Creek Inn  888-452-3182 or 608-452-3182
Closed Monday year round, and Tuesday October–May
Norskedalen Nature & Heritage Center 608-452-3424
www.norskedalen.org

**Great River Road**

www.wigreatriverroad.org
www.greatriver.com

**La Crescent**

Chamber of Commerce 800-926-9480 www.lacrescentmn.com
Applefest: 3rd weekend in September

**La Crosse**

Area Convention & Visitor's Bureau 800-658-9424
www.explorelacrosse.com
Grandad Bluff: east on Main St., follow the signs
Historic Riverside Park: block from Downtown Historic District
La Crosse Queen Paddlewheeler 608-784-2893
www.lacrossequeen.com

**Lansing**

Commercial Fish Museum/Museum of River History
563-538-4641 www.lansingiowa.com/rivermuseum.htm
Noon–4 p.m. weekends

**New Albin**

Fish Farm Mounds State Preserve 563-544-4260
www.visitiowa.org

**Westby**

Tourist Information Center—Stabbur 608-634-4011
www.westbywi.com
Round barn information & maps available

# 4  MINDORO CUT

The *Mindoro Cut* offers several hours of riding pleasure to a very unusual destination. The terrain and roads are very representative of Coulee Country, with its short, steep valleys, and long ridges.

Mindoro Cut

## NOTES & HIGHLIGHTS

A favorite road of many motorcyclists is Highway 33. Tell someone you've been in Coulee Country and they'll talk excitedly about the curves and beauty of it.

Highway 162 follows Dutch Creek along the coulee bottom. This is a well known trout stream, and I have frequently seen fly fishermen in the creek.

Bangor is a tiny town first settled in 1853 by John Wheldon and his family. If you're riding with a child on the back of the cycle, you may wonder how the Wheldon family traveled all the way across the country with seven children.

County Road DE snakes its way through and over several coulees to Mindoro. This is such a nice road you may be tempted to ride it twice.

The reason for the name of this route is located on Highway 108. The road journeys through a passage cut into the rock. At 74-feet deep and 25-feet wide, the Mindoro Cut is the second largest hand-hewn cut in the nation. There is a plaque about its construction, but the pull-off is gravel. Continue on Highway 108 as it makes several tight turns on its way along and over Severson Coulee.

West Salem was originally named Salem. When it was learned a town by that name already existed in southeastern Wisconsin, West was added.

The village owes its existence to two men. In the early 1850s Monroe Palmer of Neshonoc offered to sell land to the railroad to come through his town. But Thomas Leonard of West Salem offered his land for free. Not surprisingly, the railroad accepted Leonard's offer and the

Farming the contours

village of Neshonoc died. Many of the buildings and homes were actually moved the one mile south to West Salem.

One of these buildings was the Palmer-Gullickson Octagon House, built in 1856. It took three weeks to move, and the family lived in it the whole time. It has been owned by a succession of doctors, including Mary Lottridge, the second female doctor in the country. It is currently open to the public.

West Salem was home to Hamlin Garland, whose writing about the frontier won a Pulitzer Prize in 1921. His homestead has been restored and is also open to the public.

County Roads M and YY cross over several small streams and Bostwick Creek, which is another nice trout stream. County YY weaves its way into and out of Tollefson Coulee.

Because of its short distance and nice variation, *Mindoro Cut* may just be a route you will want to ride twice.

Farming in the valley

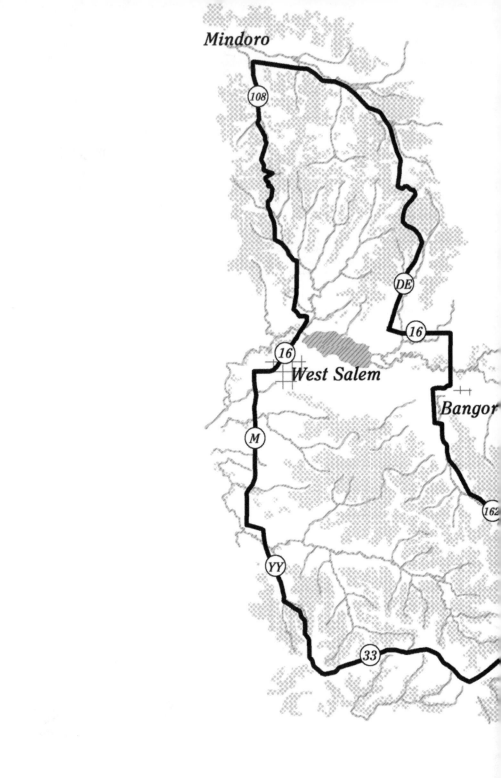

# MINDORO CUT
## 73 MILES

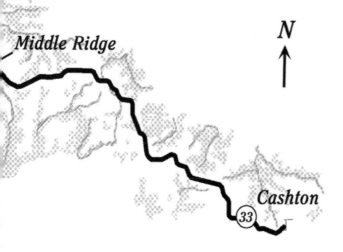

*Middle Ridge*

N

*Cashton*

33

# MINDORO CUT - 73 MILES

Start in Cashton.

| Road | Direction | | Miles |
|---|---|---|---|
| Hwy 33 | | E | 11.2 |
| Hwy 162 via Bangor | Right | N | 9.9 |
| Hwy 16 | Left | W | 1.3 |
| County DE to Mindoro | Right | N | 11.0 |
| Hwy 108 | Left | S | 9.0 |
| Hwy 16 via West Salem | Right | W | 1.8 |
| County M to Jct. with Co. O | Left | S | 4.1 |
| County M | Left | S | 0.4 |
| County YY (1st right) | Right | S | 4.9 |
| Hwy 33 | Left | E | 19.7 |

Friends along the way

# FOR MORE INFORMATION

**Cashton**

www.bikesandberries.com/cashton.html

Ages Past Country Inn & Restaurant  608-654-5950

www.agespast.net

Cashton Mercantile 608-654-5387 www.cashtonmercantile.com

Down a Country Road 608-654-5318

www.downacountryroad.com

**West Salem**

Village of West Salem 608-786-1858

www.westsalemwi.com

Hamlin Garland Homestead 608-786-1399

Memorial Day–Labor Day, 1–5

Palmer-Gullickson Octagon Home

Memorial Day–Labor Day, 1–5

---

I'll never forget my first encounter of the Interstate kind. I'd been riding about three weeks, and my friend Joyce and I went for a ride. Joyce was leading and we were heading for the freeway. I kept thinking, "She'll turn here." Nope! "Okay, here." Nope! "Oh, noooo! We're headed for the Interstate." I hung on for dear life as we went faster than I'd ever gone. And with trucks whizzing by at an even faster rate.

I prefer the back roads, but after riding through Chicago, San Diego, and Dallas in one summer, I'm feeling more comfortable on the Interstate.

# V - BARABOO HILLS
# & BEYOND

**DEVIL'S RUN - 81 MILES**
**LOOK OUT ABOVE - 182 MILES**

# V - BARABOO HILLS & BEYOND

Devil's Lake

If you had been able to ride in the Baraboo Hills or Bluffs 500 million years ago, it would have been a very short ride. Many geologists believe this "mountainous" oval was surrounded by a tropical sea near the equator. Over the years the continent moved north 10,000 miles (about an inch per year) and the sea drained. The hard quartzite rock of the Baraboo Bluffs resisted erosion, and today there is nothing like the Baraboo Hills anywhere else in the world.

Geology alone makes the hills a special place. But according to the Nature Conservancy, they are also home to one of the most outstanding ecosystems in the hemisphere. There are few forests in the Midwest that are of the size and diversity of the Baraboo Hills.

**Baraboo Hills & Beyond** lies mostly in the Driftless area, but the Wisconsin Glacier is responsible for much of its natural beauty. Devil's Lake was formed when the glacier passed over the eastern hills and blocked an ancient river valley at both ends with moraines. Beyond the Baraboo Hills to the north a large lake formed when the glacier began to melt. The lake was about the size of the Great Salt Lake and 150 feet deep. An ice dam around the Cascade Mountain area held the lake back. When this dam finally gave way, the lake dropped 100 feet in just a few days. The force of the raging water tore great channels through the sandstone to create the beauty of the Wisconsin Dells. It also washed away sediments that formed around the mesas and buttes of Adams County and left such landmarks as Quincy Bluff, Roche-A-Cri Mound and Friendship Mound. And of course, the Wisconsin River was formed.

Among the early inhabitants were Native Americans the French called Winnebagos. Beginning in the 1820s the Indians were compelled to cede their lands to the United States and then were forcibly moved across the Mississippi River. Many of the Winnebagos returned repeatedly only to be removed once again. Yellow Thunder was called "the man who would not leave" because it seemed he would return before the guard who accompanied him. In 1873 Yellow Thunder circumvented the removal policy by buying forty acres near Wisconsin Dells. His property became a gathering spot for other Winnebagos to join in powwows and dances. Soon tourists began arriving to watch, and this was the beginning of the Stand Rock Ceremonial Dances.

In 1875 the Homestead Act was changed to include Indians, and many Winnebagos began to repurchase their native land. In 1994 members of the tribe voted to renounce the French name Winnebago and return to the name they'd been calling themselves: HoChunkgra or Ho-Chunk. The Ho-Chunk Nation is now a major influence in the Baraboo Hills.

European settlers began to arrive in the area in large numbers in the 1830s. The primary draw was timber. White pine was prevalent, and good water sources were available for transporting logs and powering sawmills. As timber stands were exhausted, the Baraboo Hills became more and more dependent on tourism. The area beyond became more dependent on farming.

Wisconsin Dells is one of the oldest resort areas in the state. Newspaper accounts in 1856 reported that Kilbourn (Wisconsin Dells) was already a destination because of its natural beauty. Steamboat tours of the Wisconsin River gorges began in 1873. Today your tour boat won't be steam powered, but it may just be a WWII "duck."

Ducks are six-wheel-drive trucks that operate on land and water. They were used extensively to transport troops and supplies for beach assaults during WWII. Over 2,000 Ducks were

Scene from Lower Dells boat tour

used in the Normandy invasion on D-Day. Now these refurbished vehicles generally provide tourist transport, but they are occasionally called in for rescue operations. During the 2008 flooding of the Baraboo River, Ducks carried over 200 people to safety and helped remove debris from the dam.

You may think stores selling moccasins and fudge are a recent invention, but the first shop to sell postcards and Indian dolls opened in 1890. The Dells has it all for the tourist: water park resorts, go-kart tracks, water ski shows, Indian ceremonial dances, and boat tours above and below the dam.

Devil's Lake also has a long history of tourism. One account in 1872 put the number of visitors at 20,000, and there were already four hotels around the lake at that time. It became a state park in 1910, making it

Parfrey's Glen

one of the four oldest parks in the state. It is currently one of the busiest. By the way, there is no real consensus on whether to spell Devil's Lake with an apostrophe or without.

Because of the diversity of the terrain and the numerous attractions, **Baraboo Hills & Beyond** is an exciting place to ride. There are two routes, totaling 263 miles:

- *Devil's Run*
- *Look Out Above*

Both the routes start in Reedsburg, but each explores a different section of terrain. *Devil's Run* is in and around the Baraboo Hills. *Look Out Above* tours the glacial lake remains along the Wisconsin River. In addition, *Look Out Above* has an extremely unusual destination: an Air National Guard bombing range.

Sunflowers on County PF

Hardwood range

Merrimac ferry

# 1  DEVIL'S RUN

Parfrey's Glen

The Baraboo Hills or Bluffs are an oval bordered roughly on the north, east, and south by the Wisconsin River. *Devil's Run* takes you around and through the bluffs and across the river. It is a short run, but the roads are scenic and there are numerous places to explore off the bike.

## NOTES & HIGHLIGHTS

A shallow, stone-lined spot in the Baraboo River became a convenient place to cross the river. David C. Reed purchased two hundred acres at this place, and Reedsburg grew up because of it. The first settlers came because of the abundance of timber, and log homes were the natural choice to build. A collection of seven such homes depicting an 1890s settlement can be toured at the Pioneer Log Village and Museum. While at the museum or most anywhere in Reedsburg, you may notice the rather uncommon black squirrel. This member of the grey squirrel family is found in few places in the country.

Hop on the bike and head out Highway 33 as it sways gently into Baraboo through a gap in the Northern Range of the Baraboo Hills. No one is quite sure where the name Baraboo originated, but it is the only city in the world with that name. It has been in use at least since 1842.

The main attraction in Baraboo is the Circus World Museum, located at the former winter grounds of the Ringling Brothers Circus. Founded in 1884 by the five Ringling brothers from Baraboo, the circus wintered here for 34 years. In 1954 their attorney, John Kelly, began the museum to celebrate not only the Ringling Brothers Circus but also the 100 or so circuses that had winter quarters in Wisconsin. In 1959 the museum was given to the state and is owned by the State Historical Society. The museum is open all year, with exhibits of more than 200 restored wagons and historical memorabilia. It is in the summer, though, that the place comes to life with live circus acts under the Big Top, concerts,

Circus wagons from Circus World Museum

animal rides, and clown acts. In the past the wagons have been loaded onto flatbed railroad cars and taken to Milwaukee for the Great Circus Parade. Since 2006 the parade has been on hiatus.

Back on the road, Highway 123 becomes South Shore Road/Lake Road and snakes its way around Devil's Lake State Park. The beauty and interest of this area makes this road a pleasure to ride. If you decide to make a stop, you'll find the entrance to the park clearly marked. Devil's Lake is breathtakingly beautiful, especially seen from the top of the 500-foot bluffs. If you hike through the area, you'll notice huge rounded boulders. They are evidence of the waves and storms that pummeled the Baraboo Hills when they were surrounded by the tropical sea.

Parfrey's Glen is a unique mini-ecosystem in a quarter-mile-long rocky gorge. Park in the lot and take a walk along the mountain-like stream. The stream provided power for sawmills and grist mills from 1846 to 1876. The last owner, Robert Parfrey, left for Minnesota, and now nothing is left of his mill but the

Devil's Doorway

foundations. The glen was known to tourists from as early as 1882.

Merrimac ferry

Marsh Road meanders out of the Hills to Highway 113 in Merrimac. You'll continue east across the Wisconsin River on the free ferry, *Colsac III*. It is power driven but guided across the river on three steel cables. Getting onto the ferry may seem a bit scary, but it is easily accessible for motorcycles. This ferry has been owned by the Wisconsin Department of Transportation since 1933 and there is no fare. Prior to that there had been ferry service with some minor lapses since 1848. The first fares were 5 cents for people, 25 cents for a horse, and 40 cents for a team of oxen. So far the state has resisted lobbying from many area residents to build a bridge. Because the ferry is such a tourist attraction, the wait can be an hour in the summer. (The refreshment stand on the Merrimac side sells huge ice cream cones.) The ferry runs 24/7 from April to December, but residents and travelers have to drive to the bridge in Prairie du Sac during the winter months. Because it's such a unique experience, I hope the ferry remains.

Highway 188 loosely follows the river and is a lightly traveled loopy road heading for the bridge into Prairie du Sac. When you reach the end of the bridge, cross Main Street and continue straight on Prairie Street. This will become County Road PF. If you choose to turn left, this will take you into Prairie du Sac and, a little further down, Sauk City. Prairie du Sac is home to the Wisconsin State Cow Chip Throw in September. Thankfully, the chips are dry. Note: There are no gas stops between Prairie du Sac and Rock Springs.

County Road PF weaves and rolls through farm fields of beans and corn and bright sunflower faces. Rocky bluffs form the backdrop to this idyllic scenery. Despite the blacktop road and modern farms, I always feel like I'm riding into a prehistoric landscape.

This feeling is further enhanced by a stop at Natural Bridge State Park. You may have the park to yourself, because it is relatively

Natural Bridge State Park

unknown. A short walk takes you from a grassy open area into the woods leading to a sandstone arch that is 25-feet high and 35-feet wide. The shelter formed below is known to have been inhabited 10,000 to 12,000 years ago—at the time the glacier to the east was melting. That would mean 500 generations of Native Americans have lived in this region. Contrast that with 6 generations of white settlers. The short trail to the arch is labeled with descriptions of the Indian uses for various plants found along the trail.

Back on the road again, the route becomes more hilly and curvy. County W stands for Wow. It twists and turns through the forests and bluffs as it follows Seeley Creek. County DD is not only scenic, but in very good condition as it rolls into the tiny town of Rock Springs. There you will find a gas station, convenience store, and several places for food. Highway 154 is a fast, curving road with some wide-open vistas as it travels from one side of the North Range to the other. Highway 23 completes the loop to Reedsburg.

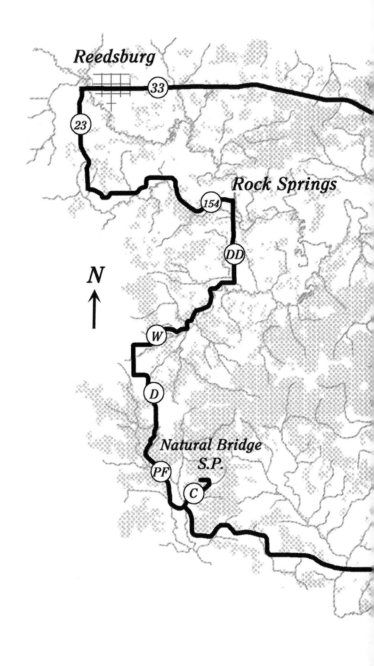

# DEVIL'S RUN
## 81 MILES

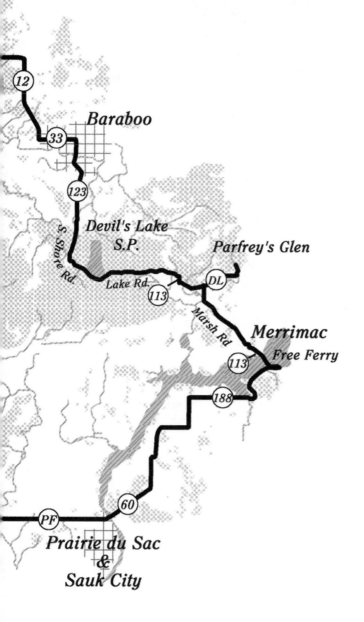

# DEVIL'S RUN - 81 MILES

Start in downtown Reedsburg.

| Road | Direction | | Miles |
|------|-----------|---|-------|
| Hwy 33 | | E | 11.5 |
| Hwy 12 | Right | S | 2.8 |
| Hwy 33 | Left | E | 1.1 |
| Hwy 123 | Right | S | 3.0 |
| S. Shore Rd./Lake Rd. | Straight | S | 5.8 |
| Devil's Lake S.P. | | | |
| Hwy 113 | Right | S | 0.4 |
| County DL | Left | E | 2.0 |
| Parfrey's Glen—marked by small brown sign | | | |
| County DL | Right | W | 1.2 |
| Marsh Rd./Cemetery Rd. | Left | N | 2.7 |
| Baraboo St. | Right | S | 0.2 |
| Hwy 113 | Left | S | 0.3 |
| Merrimac free ferry across Wisconsin River | | | |
| Hwy 188 | Right | W | 7.6 |
| Hwy 60 to Prairie du Sac | Right | W | 1.7 |
| County PF (Prairie St.) | Straight | W | 13.7 |
| County C via Leland | Right | N | 1.5 |
| Natural Bridge S.P. | | | |
| County C | Right | S | 1.5 |
| County PF | Right | N | 4.0 |
| County D | Left | N | 1.7 |
| County W | Right | N | 5.7 |
| County DD to Rock Springs | Left | N | 2.7 |
| Hwy 154 | Left | W | 6.2 |
| Hwy 23 | Right | N | 3.5 |

# FOR MORE INFORMATION

**Baraboo**

    Chamber of Commerce 800-227-2266

        www.baraboo.com

    Circus World Museum 608-356-8341

        www.wisconsinhistory.org/circusworld

        Live performances May–September, 9 a.m.–6 p.m.

    Devil's Lake State Park (state park sticker required)

        608-356-8301

        www.dnr.wi.gov/org/land/parks/specific/devilslake

        Includes Natural Bridge State Park and Parfrey's Glen Natural Area

        Additional website www.devilslakewisconsin.com

**Merrimac**

    Merrimac Ferry 608-246-3806 www.tn.merrimac.wi.gov/ferry

**Reedsburg**

    Chamber of Commerce www.reedsburg.com

    Pioneer Log Village and Museum

        Memorial Day weekend–September

        1p.m.–4p.m., weekends only

**Sauk Prairie**

    Chamber of Commerce 608-643-3544

        www.saukprairie.com

---

My scariest experience occurred in South Dakota. The road was under construction and the pilot car led traffic down an embankment onto a track carved out by an earth mover. I tried to follow the car ruts through soft black dirt and failed, burying the bike to the frame. It took three construction guys to get me out and a road grader to blade me a more solid path. It was a long two miles. I learned to ask the flagger beforehand whether I could make it through.

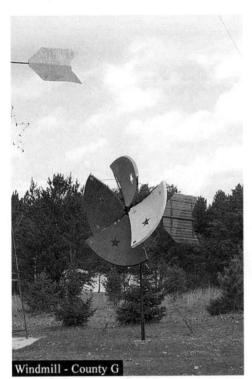
Windmill - County G

*Look Out Above* begins in the Baraboo Hills then visits the glacial lake remains along the Wisconsin River.

In the early 1800s this area was described as an unbroken wilderness. The pine forest was so dense that it stained the water of the Yellow River. Lumbering began in 1838, and by 1877 the timber stands were gone. Farmers moved onto the cleared land and further cut down woodlots and drained the swamps. Trees and wildlife both disappeared.

In the 1920s the Wisconsin River Power Company began planning dams along the Wisconsin River, and farmers along the Yellow and Wisconsin Rivers sold their lands. Because the Castle Rock Dam wasn't completed until 1940, much of the land reverted to the scrub oak and jack pine landscape of today. Deer, turkey, and other wildlife reappeared. While much of this was eventually flooded, a substantial amount remains.

The geological and historical features would be reason enough to ride this route, but the Hardwood Air to Ground Gunnery Range is the primary destination.

## NOTES & HIGHLIGHTS

As I rounded a curve on County Road H just outside Reedsburg, the Baraboo Hills laid themselves out in front of me. After all the riding I'd done up and down the valleys and hills of southwest Wisconsin, this view awed me. I've tried to describe it ever since. My words being inadequate, you will have to experience this for yourself.

County Roads H and HH twist and roll through rounded hills and forests into Lyndon Station. There are several places to stop for food.

Gas and an interstate connection is a little north of town.

From Lyndon Station the terrain begins to flatten out, and the road starts to follow the Wisconsin River. The hardwood forest makes way for stands of pine. Castle Rock County Park is a short, paved drive off County G. This lovely, well-kept park on Castle Rock Lake has a beach and camping and picnic areas. Just south is the dam that created Wisconsin's fourth largest inland lake in 1940.

County G continues north and crosses the Yellow River to a peninsula formed by the confluence of the Yellow

Castle Rock County Park

and Wisconsin Rivers. The causeway is a slow, serpentine road with a nice view of the river. Buckhorn State Park on the peninsula was designated in 1974 to promote the return of the unbroken wilderness of the early 1800s.

From the state park, the Wisconsin River begins to disappear into sloughs, backwaters, and swamps until it reaches the Petenwell Dam north of Highway 21. County G becomes straight and fast through dense pine stands.

Riding along County F into the teeny town of Findley, you may hear the screaming sound of a jet engine. Turn onto 11th Avenue at the sign, and you've arrived at the Hardwood Air to Ground Gunnery Range. I'm sorry to say, this road is dirt. But as long as it's dry, you should have no problem getting to the range. It will be bumpy, though.

The Air National Guard facility provides combat training to aircrews by the use of a variety of realistic targets such as fuel storage tanks, a scud missile launcher, bridges, and vehicles. Air National Guard and Reserve units from the Midwest and regular military air forces from throughout the United States use the range. The British Royal Air Force was there on one of my visits. Various types of aircraft fly from Volk Field near Camp Douglas, Wisconsin. Practice takes place from 17,000 feet to several hundred feet. Some of the planes are so high the only way you know they've flown over is by the puff of smoke or dust on the range from the bomb strike. Other times they're so low you can smell the fuel. The public is allowed to view the range from a spot next to the control tower and to hear the discussion between the tower and the pilot. You may be allowed into the tower, depending on the type of practice. Ask one of the ground personnel. If you are allowed, the controllers don't have much time to talk with you, and all talk is at a whisper. It's an incredible experience. Practice is held nearly every day in good weather. You can call 608-427-1509 for a recorded daily bombing schedule. Comfort facilities are limited.

An open house has been held every two years. There are F-16 cockpit displays, machine gun hands-on demonstrations, B-1Bs and

Machine gun practice - Hardwood Open House

F-16 bombing practice, F-16 gatling gun strafing demos, and a variety of other demonstrations. The open house in 1999 drew a crowd of 10,000 people, and there was special motorcycle parking. This is definitely a one-of-a-kind event.

The road north of the range is also dirt until Range Line Road, which is a nice curvy road through pine forest and cranberry bog. Wood County is the largest inland cranberry growing area in the United States, and you will see bogs along Highway 173 also. The small town of Babcock has an Ocean Spray receiving plant that holds tours mid-September through October. Many of the cranberry companies also hold tours of their bogs.

That awful smell is coming from the paper mill in Nekoosa. For those living in the area, it's the smell of money, since the mill is the biggest employer. After seeing truckloads of logs being delivered, it isn't hard to realize that the pine stands are still valuable today.

County Road Z twists and curves with the Wisconsin River south along the Petenwell Flowage, which is Wisconsin's second largest lake. The

Cranberry harvest

Petenwell Dam is one of 26 hydro plants on the Wisconsin River. From Monroe Center the road is straight and fast until the last few miles before Highway 82 where the road begins to arch and curve.

A little detour takes you to Roche-A-Cri (crevice in rock) State Park, where you'll find the 300-foot mesa for which it's named. Etched into the sandstone rock face is a record of inhabitants dating from around 100 A.D. These early petroglyphs and pictographs are joined by names and dates of early European settlers, as well as more recent tourists. The mesa stood as a landmark for early Indian traders and includes directions left by these traders. Other symbols may have religious significance, because sheer rock faces were considered doors to the spirit world. Many vision quests started here. You may have a vision quest yourself after you climb the 303 steps to the top of the mesa. On a clear day this breathtaking view extends 60 miles.

The detour takes you to the outskirts of Friendship and its sister city, Adams. If you continue south on Highway

Roche-A-Cri mesa

13 you will find the two bustling little communities. Staying on the route will take you along Friendship Mound, where Skyline Ski Hill is located.

Quincy Bluff is worth a little side trip off County Z. This secluded sandstone mesa is two miles long and 200 feet high. The Nature Conservancy and DNR are working to restore this area to the animal and plant life present when settlers first arrived in 1800.

Highway 13 can be a very busy road in the middle of tourist season. River Road is marked, but the Winnebago Indian Museum near the corner is another landmark for your turn. The Indian Museum has been owned by the Little Eagle family for 30 years and contains a large private collection of Indian artifacts. I once had an enlightening conversation about the Ho-Chunk name with the owner.

River Road is extremely scenic passing through the tight, winding gorges of the Dells. During tourist season it's also busy with people turning in and out of the resorts, restaurants, and golf course. The road ends in the heart of downtown Wisconsin Dells.

In the midst of the hustle-bustle that is the modern day Wisconsin

H. H. Bennett Studio

Dells stands the H. H. Bennett Studio and History Center. The early popularity of the Dells owes much to the tireless promotion of photographer Henry Hamilton Bennett. His equipment in the late 1800s was not the compact digital or throwaway cameras we have today. He lugged huge cameras with glass plates over rugged terrain to capture the natural beauty of the Dells. And when his photographic needs outdistanced available equipment, he invented it himself.

The stereoscope was a popular means of viewing photos in the Victorian era. Bennett developed a machine that allowed him to "mass" produce thousands of photographs, which were sold throughout the Midwest.

Bennett's granddaughter, Jean Dyer Reese, and her husband, Oliver Reese, operated the studio until donating it to the State Historical Society in 1999. The restored studio is open to the public. A special treat for the visitor is the studio store with thousands of Bennett's outstanding photographs. It is from his store that Bennett began to sell Indian crafts such as moccasins. The exhibits and photos highlight the beauty of the late-nineteenth-century Wisconsin Dells.

A short way from the Dells is the International Crane Foundation (ICF), an unusual educational and preservation facility for cranes worldwide. At this site you can see all fifteen crane species and come away with all the information you ever wanted about cranes. The ICF is engaged in captive breeding and reintroducing cranes to the wild. You can talk with human "chick parents" feeding and teaching their broods. Or observe the whooping cranes and learn how they have been saved from extinction and the efforts being made to reintroduce them to the

Whooping it up - ICF

wild. Walking the four nature trails is a relaxing way to learn the importance of habitat to the cranes' survival.

Having gone from jet planes to cranes, Highway 23 returns you to Reedsburg.

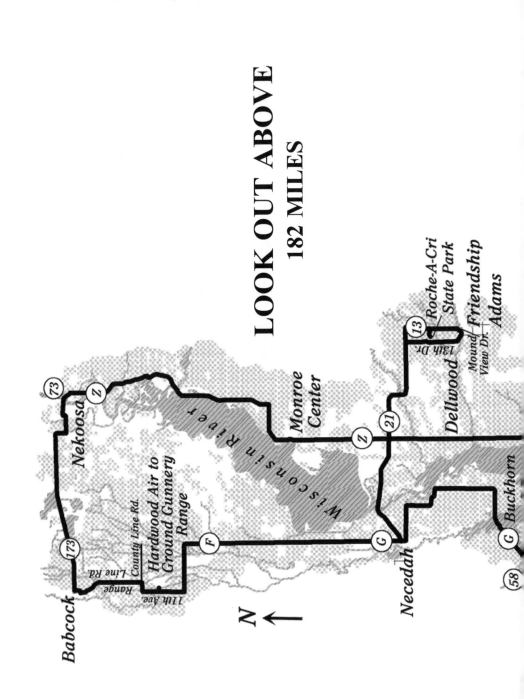

# LOOK OUT ABOVE
## 182 MILES

Babcock

Nekoosa

73

Z

173

Range Line Rd.

County Line Rd.

11th Ave.

Hardwood Air to
Ground Gunnery
Range

F

N →

Wisconsin River

Monroe
Center

Z

Z

21

Necedah

G

Dellwood

13

Roche-A-Cri
State Park

13th Dr.

Mound
View Dr.

Friendship

Adams

Buckhorn

G

58

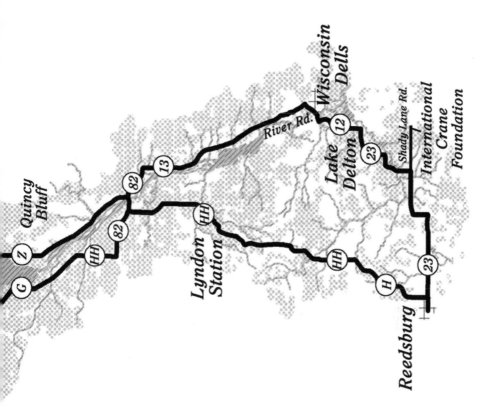

Quincy Bluff

Z

G

HH

82

82

13

River Rd.

Wisconsin Dells

12

Lake Delton

23

Shady Lane Rd.

International Crane Foundation

HH

Lyndon Station

HH

H

23

Reedsburg

# LOOK OUT ABOVE - 182 MILES

Start in downtown Reedsburg.

| Road | Direction | | Miles |
|------|-----------|---|-------|
| Hwy 23 | | E | 1.1 |
| County H | Left | N | 5.1 |
| County HH via Lyndon Station | Left | N | 14.9 |
| Hwy 82 | Left | W | 2.7 |
| County HH | Right | N | 5.4 |
| County G  to Castle Rock C.P. | Right | N | 1.2 |
| County G | Right | NE | 3.8 |
| Hwy 58 | Right | N | 1.7 |
| County G | Right | E | 22.1 |
| County F | Left | N | 5.7 |
| 11th Ave. | Right | N | 1.4 |
| | Becomes dirt road to Range Line Rd. | | |
| Hardwood Gunnery Range Entrance | | | |
| 11th Ave. | Right | N | 1.0 |
| County Line Rd. | Right | E | 0.5 |
| Range Line Rd. via Babcock | Left | N | 3.9 |
| Hwy 173 via Nekoosa | Right | E | 11.6 |
| Hwy 73 | Right | E | 0.6 |
| County Z to Monroe Center | Right | S | 16.2 |
| County Z | Straight | S | 5.6 |
| Hwy 21 | Left | E | 7.3 |
| Hwy 13 | Right | S | 1.8 |
| Roche-A-Cri S.P. | Right | W | |
| Hwy 13 | Right | S | 1.9 |
| Mound View Dr./13th Dr. | Right | N | 3.7 |
| | Just before bridge/turn off to Skyline | | |
| Hwy 21 | Left | W | 6.5 |
| County Z to Dellwood | Left | S | 3.8 |
| County Z | Straight | S | 8.4 |

| Road | Direction | | Miles |
|------|-----------|---|-------|
| | | | |

*(Quincy Bluff side trip—Hiking maps at park kiosk—Parking lot is rough and grass*

| Road | Direction | | Miles |
|------|-----------|---|-------|
| Edgewood Ave./16th Dr. | Left | E | 3.1 |

*Quincy Town Hall)*

| Road | Direction | | Miles |
|------|-----------|---|-------|
| County Z | Straight | S | 1.7 |
| Hwy 82 | Left | E | 1.9 |
| Hwy 13 | Right | S | 6.7 |
| River Rd. | Right | S | 4.6 |

Winnebago Indian Museum

| Road | Direction | | Miles |
|------|-----------|---|-------|
| Hwy 13 | Right | W | 0.6 |
| Hwy 12 | Left | S | 2.6 |
| Hwy 23 | Right | W | 4.7 |

Mirror Lake S.P. sign

| Road | Direction | | Miles |
|------|-----------|---|-------|
| Shady Lane Rd. | Left | E | 4.5 |

Cross Hwy 12
International Crane Foundation

| Road | Direction | | Miles |
|------|-----------|---|-------|
| Shady Lane Rd. | Left | W | 4.3 |
| Hwy 23 | Left | W | 9.1 |

An old-timer in my HOG® chapter named Fred gave me this tip: When you come to an intersection or driveway with a stopped vehicle, watch the tires. If the tires start to roll, the driver hasn't seen you. Be prepared to take defensive action. This tip has served me well on several occasions.

# FOR MORE INFORMATION

**Adams County**
   Chamber of Commerce 888-339-6997
      www.adamscountywi.com
   Roche-A-Cri State Park (state park sticker required)
      608-565-2789
      www.dnr.wi.gov/org/land/parks/specific/roche-a-cri

**Baraboo**
   Chamber of Commerce 800-227-2266
      www.baraboo.com
   International Crane Foundation 608-356-9462
      www.savingcranes.org

**Hardwood Air to Ground Gunnery Range**
      608-427-1509 Recording of daily bombing schedule
      (not always current)
      www.globalsecurity.org/military/facility/
      hardwood.htm

**Juneau County**
   Chamber of Commerce 608-427-2070
      www.juneaucounty.com
   Buckhorn State Park (state park sticker required)
      608-565-2789
      www.dnr.wi.gov/org/land/parks/specific/buckhorn

**Necedah**
      www.necedah.us 608-565-2261
   Necedah Wildlife Refuge 608-565-2551
      www.fws.gov/midwest/Necedah
      www.gorp.com/gorp/resource/us_nwr/wi_neced.htm
   Operation Migration 800-675-2618
      www.operationmigration.org
      (training whooping cranes at NWR for ultralight
      led migration to Florida)

## Nekoosa

www.nekoosa.org

Wisconsin Rapids Area Convention & Visitors' Bureau
800-554-4484 www.visitwisrapids.com

## Reedsburg

Chamber of Commerce www.reedsburg.com

Pioneer Log Village and Museum

Memorial Day weekend–September

1p.m.–4p.m., weekends only

## Wisconsin Dells

Visitor's Bureau 800-223-3557 or 608-254-8088

www.dellschamber.com

H. H. Bennett Studio & History Center 608-253-3523

www.wisconsinhistory.org/hhbennett

May–October daily, fee

November–April weekends only; closed January

Crane fly-in at ICF

# PHOTO CREDITS

All photographs taken by the author except the following:

# MOTORCYCLE DEALER LISTING

Listed alphabetically by city

Johnson Sales, Inc.
  N1255 US Highway 51
  **Arlington**, Wisconsin 53911
  608-635-7381
Don & Roy's Cycle Shop
  17740 W. Bluemound Rd.
  **Brookfield**, Wisconsin 53045
  262-786-3220
Cedar Creek Motorsports
  7518 State Highway 60
  **Cedarburg**, Wisconsin 53012
  262-377-5700
Maxxx Motorsports
  690 Gerry Way
  **Darien**, Wisconsin 53114
  262-882-6299
Arrowhead Motorsports
  363 Austin Cir.
  **Delafield**, Wisconsin 53018
  262-646-5335
Sportsman's Park
  3552 State Road 50
  **Delavan**, Wisconsin 53115
  262-728-6037
Sindt Motor Sales, Inc.
  4460 Dodge St.
  **Dubuque**, Iowa 52003
  563-582-8146
Wilwert's Harley-Davidson
  145 N. Crescent Ridge
  **Dubuque**, Iowa 52003
  563-557-8040

Cycles Plus, Inc.
  701 N. Lincoln St.
  **Elkhorn**, Wisconsin 53121
  262-723-5518
Petrie Motorsports
  950 County H
  **Elkhorn**, Wisconsin 53121
  262-723-5518
Freeport Kawasaki
  3086 Route 26 N.
  **Freeport**, Illinois 61032
  815-235-7549
Wilwerts H-D of Galena
  939 Galena Square Dr.
  **Galena**, Illinois 61036
  815-777-9800
Hartford Harley-Davidson
  427 Sumner St. (Hwy. 60)
  **Hartford**, Wisconsin 53027
  262-670-1000
Rock River Powersports
  365 E. Racine St.
  **Jefferson**, Wisconsin 53549
  920-674-9280
Ace Powersports
  8124 S. Sheridan Rd.
  **Kenosha**, Wisconsin 53143
  262-654-3090
Uke's Harley-Davidson
  5999 120th Ave.
  **Kenosha**, Wisconsin 53144
  262-652-3653
Johnson Sales & Service
  1922 West Ave. S.
  **La Crosse**, Wisconsin 54601
  608-784-6444

Steiger Kawasaki Suzuki
    4140 Mormon Coulee Ct.
    **La Crosse**, Wisconsin 54601
    608-788-4514
Two Brothers Honda
    124 Rose St.
    **La Crosse**, Wisconsin 54603
    608-781-3360
Midwest Action Cycle, Inc.
    251 Host Dr.
    **Lake Geneva**, Wisconsin 53147
    414-249-0600
Bob Barr's Kawasaki
    1701 S. Stoughton Rd.
    **Madison**, Wisconsin 53716
    608-222-6800
Capital City Harley-Davidson
    6200 Millpond Rd.
    **Madison**, Wisconsin 53718
    608-221-2761
Engelhart Sports Center
    1589 Greenway Cross
    **Madison**, Wisconsin 53713
    608-274-2366
Sutter's Speed Shop
    3333 Femrite Dr.
    **Madison**, Wisconsin 53718
    608-221-8865
Cliff Eckes' Cycle Service
    S. 2979 Schmidt Rd.
    **Marshfield**, Wisconsin, 54449
    715-384-4555
Crafts Trading Center Inc.
    10566 S. Washington Ave.
    **Marshfield**, Wisconsin 54449
    715-591-1000

Power Pac, Inc.
    10599 State Highway 13
    **Marshfield**, Wisconsin 54449
    715-387-1106
Bala's Harley-Davidson, Inc.
    N 4833 Highway 58
    **Mauston**, Wisconsin 53948
    608-847-7702
BMW Motorcycles of Milwaukee
    7016 N. 76th St.
    **Milwaukee**, Wisconsin 53223
    414-358-2465
Cycle Empire
    4001 W. Loomis Rd.
    **Milwaukee**, Wisconsin 53221
    414-325-8747
House of Harley-Davidson Airport Store
    5300 S. Howell Ave.
    **Milwaukee**, Wisconsin 53207
    414-747-4703
House of Harley-Davidson, Inc.
    6221 W. Layton Ave.
    **Milwaukee**, Wisconsin 53220
    414-282-2211/877-518-4643
Kawasaki of Milwaukee
    6930 N. 76th St.
    **Milwaukee**, Wisconsin 53223
    414-463-2540
Milwaukee Harley-Davidson
    11310 Silver Spring Rd.
    **Milwaukee**, Wisconsin 53225
    414-461-4444
Hauris Cycle Shop
    633 1st Ave.
    **Monroe**, Wisconsin 53566
    608-325-9952

Kutter Harley-Davidson
   129 W. 6th St.
   **Monroe**, Wisconsin 53566
   608-329-4884
Monroe Honda
   502 10th St.
   **Monroe**, Wisconsin 53566
   608-325-3071
Hal's Harley-Davidson, Inc.
   1925 Moorland Rd.
   **New Berlin**, Wisconsin 53151
   262-860-2060
Sportland 2, Inc.
   7331 S. 13th St.
   **Oak Creek**, Wisconsin 53154
   414-764-2800
Wisconsin Harley-Davidson, Inc.
   1280 Blue Ribbon Dr.
   **Oconomowoc**, Wisconsin 53066
   262-569-8500
La Crosse Area Harley-Davidson
   1116 Oak Forest Dr.
   **Onalaska**, Wisconsin 54650
   608-783-6112
Puma's Custom Cycles
   1129 Washington Ave.
   **Racine**, Wisconsin 53403
   262-637-1313
Racine Harley-Davidson
   1155 Oakes Rd.
   **Racine**, Wisconsin 53406
   262-884-0123
Racine Motor Sports
   2005 Lathrop Ave.
   **Racine**, Wisconsin 53405
   262-632-4000

Shoreline Motorsports Kawasaki
  321 Sheridan Rd.
  **Racine**, Wisconsin 53403
  262-552-7911
New World Sports Kawasaki
  28526 US Highway 14
  **Richland Center**, Wisconsin 53581
  608-647-4131
Vetesnik Motors, Inc.
  27475 US Highway 14
  **Richland Center**, Wisconsin 53581
  608-647-8808
Sauk Prairie Harley-Davidson, Inc.
  836 Phillips Blvd.
  **Sauk City**, Wisconsin 53583
  608-643-3735
Route 43 Harley-Davidson
  3736 South Taylor Dr.
  **Sheboygan**, Wisconsin 53081
  920-458-0777
Sheboygan Yamaha
  N7402 Highway 42
  **Sheboygan**, Wisconsin 53083
  920-565-2213
Thomson Honda
  5425 Race Track Rd.
  **Sheboygan**, Wisconsin 53081
  920-457-8855
Lil Scott's Customs
  2920 Wisconsin St.
  **Sturtevant**, Wisconsin 53177
  262-884-9155
Suburban Motors
  139 North Main St.
  **Thiensville**, Wisconsin 53092
  262-242-2464

Leisure Time Sports
1705 Winnnebago Ave.
**Tomah**, Wisconsin, 54660
608-372-5939

BMW Motorcycles of Milwaukee
3000 Pleasant Valley Rd.
**West Bend**, Wisconsin 53095
262-677-0396

Glenn Curtiss Motorsports
4345 Highway 33
**West Bend**, Wisconsin 53095
262-338-3684

Mid-Cities Motorsports
7515 Friendly Dr.
**West Bend**, Wisconsin 53095
262-338-1118

West Bend Harley-Davidson
2910 W. Washington St.
**West Bend**, Wisconsin 53095
262-338-8761

Bala's Harley-Davidson of Wisconsin Dells
524 Wisconsin Dells Pkwy.
**Wisconsin Dells**, Wisconsin 53965
608-253-2252

Country Sports, Inc.
10520 Highway 13 S.
**Wisconsin Rapids**, Wisconsin 54494
715-325-5381

Donahue Super Sports
6821 Plover Rd.
**Wisconsin Rapids**, Wisconsin 54494
715-424-1762

Neinfeldt's Cycle
4811 Plover Rd.
**Wisconsin Rapids,** Wisconsin 54494
715-423-1903

Barbara Barber bought her first motorcycle in 1997. Since that time she has ridden over 200,000 miles on five different bikes. She is currently a member of the Kenosha and Black River Falls Chapters of the Harley Owners Group®. She resides in west central Wisconsin.